Dr Allison Waters and Dr Trisha Groth

The Take Action Program

A User-Friendly Cognitive-Behavioural Therapy Program for Practitioners Working with Anxious Children

Take Action Practitioner Guidebook

www.
AUSTRALIANACADEMICPRESS
.com.au

Other titles in the Take Action program:
Take Action Child Handout Workbook
Take Action Parent Handout Workbook

Take Action Practitioner Guidebook
First published 2016
Australian Academic Press Group Pty. Ltd.
18 Victor Russell Drive
Samford Valley QLD 4520
Australia
www.australianacademicpress.com.au

ISBN 9781922117274

Cover design by Maria Biaggini of The Letter Tree

Text design and typesetting by Australian Academic Press

Cartoons and illustrations by Karen Mounsey-Smith of Gidgeymo Illustrations

Acknowledgments

To Sanchia, Darren, Dayne and Merryn — with all my thanks for your love and support.

AMW

To Joel, Amia and Luke — with all my love.

TAG

This Practitioner Guide is based on the Take Action program, developed by Dr Waters and Dr Groth. This program has been influenced by many group facilitators, and children and parents who have received treatment. We thank everyone who has contributed to the development of the program over the past ten years.

AMW and TAG

Who can use Take Action?

The evidence-base for the Take Action Program has been established with the Program being delivered by registered psychologists, clinical psychologists, school psychologists and school guidance counsellors who are trained and experienced in Cognitive-Behavioural Therapy (CBT). Therefore, the Take Action Program is recommended for use by these mental health and educational professionals. The *Take Action Child Handout Workbook* and the *Take Action Parent Handout Workbook* should be used with children and parents only in conjunction with this accompanying *Take Action Practitioner Guidebook.* The practitioner guidebook and child and parent handout workbooks have been developed for practitioners to use when working with anxious children and their parents. They are not to be reproduced in any form for teaching, training, or educational purposes (including but not limited to handouts or slides for lectures and workshops).

Contents

Acknowledgments .... **iii**

Who can use Take Action? .... **iv**

About the Authors .... **viii**

Introduction to the Take Action Program

What is Take Action? 1

Anxiety Disorders in Children 1

Causes and Maintenance of Anxiety Disorders in Children 4

An Integrative Framework for Understanding the Causes and Maintenance of Childhood Anxiety Disorders 9

References 10

How to use this Practitioner Guide

Organisation of this Guide 17

Aims of take Action 17

Anxiety Disorders Covered by Take Action 18

Age Appropriateness for Take Action 20

What does the ACTION in Take Action stand for? 21

How Take Action Works with the 3-Response-System of Anxiety 21

Introducing the Sea Animals 21

Using Take Action with Groups and Individuals 22

Using Take Action in Schools 24

Parent Involvement in Take Action 25

Practitioner Skills Required for Take Action 25

Practitioner Checklist 26

References 27

Assessment Module

Major Activities in this Module 31

Rapport Building and Socialisation to Treatment 31

Diagnosis 32
Diagnostic Interviews 32
Questionnaire Measures 34
Program Evaluation 36
References 36
Evaluation Sheet 1 39
Evaluation Sheet 2 40

Treatment Modules

Module 1.1 Introduction to a Take Action Group 43
Module 1.2 A – Be AWARE 45
Module 2 C – Keep CALM 53
Module 3 T – THINK Strong Thoughts 59
Module 4 I – Get INTO Action 69
Module 5 O – Use my OPTIONS 77
Module 6 N – NEVER Stop Taking ACTION 89

Considerations when Working with Children who have Comorbid Conditions 93

Trouble Shooting 95

Appendix A — Child Handouts

Module 1 Introduction and Be Aware 1–14 ..... AA 1
Module 2 Keep Calm 1–5 ..... AA 19
Module 3 Thoughts 1–14 ..... AA 25
Module 4 Into Action 1–5 ..... AA 41
Module 5 Options 1–16 ..... AA 47
Module 6 Never Stop 1–8 ..... AA 67

Appendix B — Parent Handouts

Module 1 Be Aware 1–15 ..... AB 1
Module 2 Keep Calm 1–3 ..... AB 17
Module 3 Strong Thoughts 1–2 ..... AB 21
Module 4 Into Action 1–3 ..... AB 25
Module 5 Options 1 ..... AB 29

Appendix C — Home Task Sheets

Home Task Reward Chart ..... AC 1
Home Task One ..... AC 2
Home Task Two ..... AC 3
Home Task Three ..... AC 4
Home Task Parent ..... AC 5
Home Task Four ..... AC 7
Home Task Five ..... AC 9
Home Task Six ..... AC 11
Home Task Seven ..... AC 12
Home Task Eight ..... AC 13
Home Task Nine ..... AC 14

About the Authors

Dr Allison Waters
BSS(Psych), BA(Hons), PhD(Clin), MAPS, MCCP

Dr Waters is Associate Professor in Clinical Psychology at Griffith University. She completed a Bachelor of Social Science (Psychology) at The Queensland University of Technology, a Bachelor of Arts and a PhD in Clinical Psychology at The University of Queensland, and a Post-Doctoral Research Fellowship at the University of California, Los Angeles. Dr Waters runs the Childhood Anxiety Disorders Research Program at Griffith University through which more than 450 children have been assessed and treated. She has published over 75 peer-reviewed book chapters and journal articles, and her research is funded by national grant funding organisations. She serves as an Associate Editor of national and international psychology journals, resides on the research advisory committees of local research institutes, and has received several awards in recognition of her research. Dr Waters supervises the research projects and clinical work of postgraduate students in clinical psychology, and teaches at the undergraduate and postgraduate levels at Griffith University. She maintains a small private practice and is a member of the Australian Psychological Society College of Clinical Psychologists and the Australian Association for Cognitive and Behavioural Therapy.

Dr Trisha Groth
BPsych(Hons), DPsych(Clin), MAPS, MCCP

Dr Groth is a clinical psychologist who specialises in the assessment and treatment of anxiety disorders in children and adolescents. She received First Class Honours in Psychology at Griffith University in 2002. She completed her Doctorate of Clinical Psychology at Griffith University in 2006. Dr Groth has practiced for ten years on the Gold Coast, working with children individually and in groups across a variety of educational, government and community settings. She is the Clinic Director of Take Action Psychology on the Gold Coast. She primarily works with children experiencing separation or generalised anxiety, social worries, and specific fears/phobias. She provides individual and group treatment to children, adolescents and their families. Dr Groth is a member of the Australian Psychological Society College of Clinical Psychologists, and the Australian Association for Cognitive and Behavioural Therapy.

Introduction to the *Take Action* Program

What is *Take Action*?

Take Action is a Cognitive Behavioural Therapy (CBT) program specifically developed with the following goals in mind:

(a) To optimise treatment outcomes through the integration of findings from recent research on the threat-based cognitive biases and maladaptive thinking styles associated with anxiety disorders in children.

(b) To provide an evidence-based cognitive-behavioural treatment program for anxious children that is practitioner-friendly.

(c) To provide a program that can be delivered in a flexible, adaptable way to suit the setting in which it is being delivered and the individual needs of children receiving treatment.

The program consists of six treatment modules for children with supporting information guidelines for parents, and one assessment module. Each session lasts approximately 1 hour. The program covers the major components of CBT including psychoeducation, somatic management, cognitive restructuring, and exposure therapy, as well as problem-solving, social skills development, strategies for being assertive, and relapse prevention and maintenance. The program can be delivered in a group or individual format for children between 4 and 12 years of age, and includes this comprehensive practitioner manual outlining how to run the child and parent sessions as well as individual handouts for children and parents. More than 450 children have completed Take Action since 2004 with research results showing that between 60–80% of children are no longer meeting criteria for their main anxiety disorder at the end of a group program. Program delivery continues to be assessed through questionnaires completed by parents, children and practitioners.

In school settings, Take Action has also been used in a flexible format by registered psychologists and school guidance counsellors who identify children in need of treatment. The program is adapted by the guidance counsellors and psychologists as deemed necessary to meet the needs of the children referred for treatment within each school. For example it might entail reducing the number of sessions to fit within the school term, combining parent- and child-sessions or sending parent-handouts home with children for parents who work and are unable to attend the sessions. The program has also been delivered classroom-wide by trained psychologists, where high levels of anxiety among children have been identified by guidance counsellors.

Anxiety Disorders in Children

Symptom Dimensions of Anxiety Disorders

Anxiety can be defined as an emotional reaction arising from a real or perceived threat and is generally conceptualised as consisting of physiological, cognitive and behavioural responses (Craske & Waters, 2005). Physiologically, anxiety is defined by heightened autonomic arousal (e.g. increased heart rate and perspiration) and somatic complaints (e.g. headaches or stomach aches). Behaviourally, anxiety is characterised by avoidance or escape, restlessness or repetitive behaviours or rituals. Cognitive features of anxiety include hypervigilance for threat, danger-laden thoughts, worry, and persistent intrusive thoughts. Although anxiety is considered a part of normal human development and is adaptive in some circumstances, fear and anxiety can become so intense that it can affect a child's functioning and psychosocial development. In these cases, anxiety may be considered as 'clinically significant' and qualify for a diagnosis.

Anxiety disorders are described and classified in diagnostic systems such as the Diagnostic and Statistical Manual of Mental Disorders (DSM, American Psychiatric Association, 2013). Most anxiety disorders share common features of physiological symptoms, avoidance, and distress/impairment in functioning, whereas the focus of anxiety varies between disorders. Diagnoses in children include separation anxiety disorder, social phobia, specific phobia, generalised anxiety disorder, post-traumatic stress disorder/acute stress disorder, panic disorder, and agoraphobia. In the fifth edition of the DSM (2013), obsessive-compulsive disorder is included in a new chapter on Obsessive-Compulsive and Related Disorders. With the exception of separation anxiety disorder, the DSM employs the same diagnostic criteria for classifying anxiety disorders in youth as in adults.

Prevalence and Course of Anxiety Disorders

Anxiety disorders are one of the most common forms of psychopathology in children, with prevalence estimates ranging from 3–25% (Cartwright-Hatton, McNicol, & Doubleday, 2006). Amongst the anxiety disorders, specific phobia and separation anxiety disorder tend to onset in early to middle childhood and decrease in prevalence by mid-adolescence (Breton et al., 1999; Kashani & Orvaschel, 1990), whereas rates of social phobia and obsessive-compulsive disorder appear to increase in late childhood through mid-adolescence, followed by panic disorder in late-adolescence to early adulthood (Ford, Goodman, & Meltzer, 2003; Kessler et al., 2005). Studies of generalised anxiety disorder tend to conclude impairment as being "lifelong" (Rapee, 1997) and involving little change with age from childhood through adulthood (Breton et al., 1999; Ford et al., 2003; Kessler et al., 2005). Moreover, childhood anxiety disorders often predate other forms of psychopathology in adolescence and adulthood, particularly other anxiety disorders and depression (e.g., Bittner et al., 2007; Pine, Guyer, & Leibenluft, 2008).

Correlates of Anxiety Disorders

Anxiety disorders in children can adversely impact children's academic, social, and vocational outcomes (e.g., Ginsburg, La Greca, & Silverman, 1998). Anxious children may have fewer friends on average than non-anxious children (Strauss, Lahey, Frick, Frame, & Hynd, 1988), may be liked less by their peers (Verduin & Kendall,

2007), and have poorer social skills (Spence, Donovan, & Brechman-Toussaint, 1999). Anxious adolescent girls are more likely to drop out of school, and adolescent boys and girls with social anxiety may be more likely to fail to enter and complete tertiary studies (Kessler, Foster, Saunders, & Stang, 1995).

Anxiety in childhood is also associated with significant health problems, including sleep difficulties (Hudson, Gradisar, Gamble, Schniering, & Rebelo, 2009), headache and somatic complaints (Masi, Favilla, Millepiedi, & Mucci, 2000) and a higher incidence of gastrointestinal symptoms than in non-anxious children (Waters, Schilpzand, Bell, Walker, & Baber, 2013).

Furthermore, childhood anxiety impacts children's general quality of life and causes considerable interference and disruption to family life; restricting family outings and holidays and the quality of parent relationships, and contributes to differences in parenting style and accommodation of anxious and non-anxious siblings (Hudson & Rapee, 2009).

Differential Diagnosis and Comorbidity

Clinically significant anxiety can be differentiated from normal childhood fears and anxiety by the severity of the anxiety, pervasiveness of distress and avoidance and the degree of interference in functioning (Albano, Causey, & Carter, 2001). Anxiety disorders can be distinguished from one another by the focus of the child's anxiety (Albano et al., 2001).

Comorbidity is common among children with anxiety disorders in clinical and community samples (Curry, March, & Hervey, 2004). In most studies, around 80% of children receiving treatment for anxiety disorders will have at least one other anxiety disorder (e.g., Last, Strauss, & Francis, 1987). High rates of comorbidity exist between generalised anxiety disorder, separation anxiety disorder, specific phobia, and social phobia. Other anxiety disorders (agoraphobia, panic disorder, obsessive-compulsive disorder and posttraumatic or acute stress disorder) have a less clear-cut comorbidity, which may be due to their relatively low prevalence rates (Costello, Egger, & Angold, 2004). Patterns of comorbidity do not appear to differ between boys and girls or between older and younger children (Craske & Waters, 2005).

Anxiety disorders in children also co-occur with other psychological disorders including depression, oppositional-defiant disorder, conduct disorder, attention-deficit/hyperactivity disorder, and substance use in older youths (Costello, Egger, & Angold, 2004). Distinguishing anxiety disorders from other childhood difficulties is more important for effective treatment than differentiating between anxiety disorders.

Gender Differences

Community studies show girls report more fears than boys between 9 and 12 years of age (King et al., 1989), and studies of 6 to 16 year olds show girls compared with boys experience higher levels of anxiety and worry (Campbell & Rapee, 1994; Rose & Rudolph, 2006). Gender differences appear to hold for anxiety diagnoses as well (e.g., Anderson, Williams, McGee, & Silva, 1987), with the exception of separation anxiety disorder (Velez, Johnson, & Cohen, 1989). However, the female propensity for anxiety diagnoses appears to be most pronounced by adolescence with fewer gender differences observed in pre-adolescent clinical samples (see Craske, 2003 for a review).

Nevertheless, this gender difference is not necessarily observed in many child anxiety clinics, where referrals for anxious boys and girls appear to be fairly similar. The reasons for this remain unclear, although as fear and anxiety stereotypically are less desirable in boys than girls, parents may be less accepting of anxiety in their son and seek treatment for them sooner (Craske, 2003).

Causes and Maintenance of Anxiety Disorders in Children

Genetic Factors

Based on the wealth of genetic studies over the past 2 decades, there is little doubt that there is a genetic basis to anxiety. Findings from twin studies suggest that genetics account for approximately 50% of the variance in anxiety symptoms (see Rapee, Schniering, & Hudson, 2009 for a review). The effects of genetics are most prominently observed in temperament; with research suggesting that around 30–50% of the variance in temperament is mediated by genetic factors (Rapee, 2002).

Intergenerational studies also provide support for the role of genetics, with parental anxiety being one of the strongest predictors of childhood anxiety with a moderate to strong concordance of anxiety type in families (Hettema, Neale & Kendler, 2001; Rapee, 2001; 2002). There is particularly strong evidence for the aggregation of panic disorder, generalized anxiety disorder, obsessive compulsive disorder and phobias within families, with the strongest evidence for panic disorder (Biederman et al., 2001; Hettema et al., 2001). Paternal anxiety has been found to confer the same risk as maternal anxiety (Connell & Goodman, 2002). Parental depression is also a risk factor for child anxiety. Findings from longitudinal studies suggest that offspring of parents with a past or current depression diagnosis are at a 2-6 times increased risk for developing an anxiety disorder (Colletti et al., 2009; Weissman et al., 2006).

Nevertheless, the evidence does not suggest that there are specific anxiety disorder genes (Andrews, 1996; Torgensen, 1983). Rather, what is probably a more important question arising from genetics research is *what* is actually inherited? Because the genetic basis for anxiety appears to be general to all anxiety disorders to varying degrees, researchers propose that what is probably inherited is a general level of negative emotionality, or differences in the extent to which each person will respond with high levels of emotional distress to various situations (Craske & Waters, 2005).

Temperament Factors

A wealth of research on the role of temperament indicates that a child who is genetically predisposed to experience anxiety may display behaviour consistent with a temperament style of "behavioural inhibition" (BI). Behavioural inhibition is characterised by fearfulness, shyness, restraint, withdrawal and proximity seeking to safety figures when faced with novel stimuli (Murray, Creswell, & Cooper, 2009). Behavioural inhibition has been found to be relatively stable, with approximately 50% of children identified as behaviourally inhibited in infancy remaining so throughout childhood (Kagan, Reznick, Snidman, Gibbons, & Johnson, 1988) and adolescence (Kagan, Snidman, Valikahn, & Towsley, 2007). Moreover, BI has been related to an increased risk for childhood anxiety disorders, particularly Social Phobia (e.g. Hirshfeld-Becker et al., 2007; Muris, van Brakel, Arntz, & Schouten, 2011).

Children with BI have also been found to have greater autonomic reactivity, elevated morning cortisol levels, heightened startle responses, and more vigilant attention styles, and heightened amygdala activation in the brain (Perez-Edgar & Fox, 2005; Perez-Edgar et al., 2007). Nevertheless, while research has shown that a large part of the variance in BI is genetically determined, environmental factors are also important. Moreover, not all children with BI go on to develop an anxiety disorder (Kagan & Snidman, 1999; Prior, Smart, Sanson, & Obkerlaid, 2000). It is estimated that between 9 and 30% of children with BI develop an anxiety disorder (e.g. Biederman et al., 1990; Prior et al., 2000). Thus, whilst BI may represent one risk factor for anxiety, it is likely to interact with other child and environmental factors in the development of anxiety disorders in children.

Parental Factors

Parental influences on children's anxiety have also received considerable research attention. However, evidence for and against the role of parenting factors has been mixed. Factors that have received the most research attention include parental over-control and lack of parental warmth. (DiBartolo & Helt, 2007; McLeod, Wood, & Weisz, 2007; Wood, McLeod, Sigman, Hwang, & Chu, 2003). Parental over-control refers to excessive regulation of a child's activities and routines in addition to discouraging child independence. Over-control may convey messages to the child that the world is a dangerous place, which may reduce the child's sense of competence and mastery and may reinforce avoidance as a way of coping with challenges (Chorpita & Barlow, 1998).

Moreover, parenting practices may be exacerbated by parental anxiety (beyond the role of heritability). Parental anxiety may interfere with the development of parents' adaptive coping skills and lead to anxiety enhancing parent-child interactions (Ginsburg, Grover, & Lalongo, 2004). Parental anxiety may exert its effect through social learning processes, due to the modelling of anxious/avoidant behaviour (e.g., Gerull & Rapee, 2002) and the transmission of anxious cognitions (Field & Cartwright-Hatton, 2008). Beyond the influence of parental psychopathology, child anxiety may exacerbate distress in parents, who then adjust demands, expectations and parenting style, and thus, negatively reinforce children's anxiety (Kendall & Ollendick, 2004).

Research examining parent-child interactions in child anxiety has identified high parental over-protection and less autonomy granting, as well as low maternal warmth/ parental rejection as key parenting factors in childhood anxiety disorders (Rapee et al., 2009). Of the two styles of parenting, the largest effect sizes and most consistent results have come from evaluation of overprotective parenting (Rapee 1997; Wood, McLeod, Sigman, Hwang, & Chu, 2003). However, the *causal* role of these practices in the development of child anxiety is unclear. Whaley, Pinto, and Sigman (1999) found anxious mothers showed less autonomy granting, less warmth, and greater criticism during interactions with their children. However, Moore, Whaley, and Sigman (2004) showed that the presence of child anxiety, but not maternal anxiety, was linked to less autonomy granting and lower warmth. Hudson, Doyle, and Gar (2009) found mothers were more involved with anxious children, even when biologically-unrelated to them, in comparison to nonclinical children. Overall, large-scale reviews of the parenting literature suggest that parenting styles account for about only 4% of the variance in childhood anxiety disorders (McLeod et al., 2007). These findings highlight the *reciprocal interaction* between child and parent factors in the development of anxiety, and the complex interplay of factors that contributes to the development and maintenance of these disorders.

Traumatic and Stressful Life Events

The role of negative life events in the development of childhood anxiety is based on associative models of fear learning which suggests that fears develop from the repeated pairing of a neutral stimulus (a dog) with an aversive event (a bite) (see Boschen, Neumann, & Waters, 2009 for a review). Research suggests that direct fear conditioning experiences are a major factor underlying the acquisition of fears amongst school-age children (Muris, Merckelbach, & Collaris, 1997). Moreover, other studies show that anxious children are more likely to have experienced a greater number and impact of negative life events compared to non-anxious children (e.g. Goodyer & Altham, 1991). Furthermore, anxious children have been found to experience more negative events in the year preceding the onset of an anxiety disorder (e.g. Allen, Rapee, & Sandberg, 2008).

However, findings from twin studies suggest that the association between negative life events and childhood anxiety is not completely genetically mediated, with an anxious twin being more likely to report independent negative events in comparison to their non-anxious twin (Eley & Stevenson, 2000). Thus, not all children will develop anxiety as a result of negative life events. This highlights that some children are more prone to acquire or learn their fears through forming associations between neutral stimuli and aversive events than other children, once again highlighting the complex interplay of various child and environmental factors in the development and maintenance of childhood anxiety disorders.

Cognitive Factors

There is well-established evidence that anxious children display a number of differences in the processes and content of their thoughts compared to non-anxious children. Guided by prominent cognitive theories of anxiety (Mogg & Bradley, 1998; Williams, Watts, MacLeod, & Mathews, 1997), studies have shown that anxious children show biases in the orientation of attention to threat stimuli and tend to interpret neutral and benign situations as overly threatening.

Attention to Threat

Increased attention to threat serves as an adaptive function in all humans for promoting safety and well-being in situations of genuine threat. However, threat-based attention biases have been observed in most types of clinical anxiety disorders (see Bar-Haim, Lamy, Pergamin, Bakermans-Kranenburg, & Van-Ijzendoorn, 2007 for a review) and anxious children have been found to disproportionately direct attention to threat stimuli compared to non-anxious children (see Waters, Farrell, Schilpzand, 2013 for a review). However, research in this area has found that whilst some anxious children direct attention towards threat, others display attentional avoidance, with attention being directed away from threat (Salum et al., 2013; Waters, Bradley, & Mogg, 2014). Moreover, avoidance of threat assessed prior to commencing cognitive-behavioural treatments has been linked to poorer treatment outcomes than anxious adults and children who show threat vigilance (Niles, Mesri, Burkland, Lieberman, & Craske, 2013; Price, Tone, & Anderson, 2011; Waters, Mogg, & Bradley, 2012).

The precise mechanisms underlying this differential response to treatment in threat avoidant anxious children are not clear. However, by virtue of being avoidant, these children may not be as well engaged in treatment or perhaps are less able to establish new learning as anxious children who direct attention towards threat. Therefore, it may be important during therapy to monitor children's visual attention and encourage greater engagement with exposure stimuli and activities in children who display avoidance.

Overestimation and Interpretation of Threat

A considerable literature has developed indicating that anxious children interpret ambiguous or mildly aversive situations as more dangerous compared to non-anxious children (e.g. Barrett, Dadds, Rapee, & Ryan, 1996; Creswell, Schniering, & Rapee, 2005; Waters, Wharton, Zimmer-Gembeck, & Craske, 2008; Waters, Craske, Bergman, & Treanor, 2008). Moreover, recent evidence indicates that threat interpretation biases improve following cognitive-behavioural therapy in children with anxiety disorders (Waters, Wharton et al., 2008). Thus, cognitive biases in the form of biased orienting of attention towards or away from threat and threat-based interpretation biases play important roles in the development and maintenance of anxiety disorders in children and affect treatment outcomes.

Brain Structure, Neuroimaging and Neurochemical Studies

Our understanding of the brain structures and circuitry implicated in childhood anxiety disorders is emerging slowly. This is due to numerous factors including methodological constraints on assessing underlying mechanisms in children, and until recently, an absence of theoretical frameworks that integrate relationships among brain circuits, psychological processes and anxiety (Waters, Farrell, & Schilpzand, 2013). Also, the uniquely plastic state of the maturing brain requires large-scale studies of a wide age range of youth which are yet to be undertaken.

Amygdala-prefrontal Cortex Circuitry

Given the strong association between threat attention bias and anxiety across the lifespan, recent research has focused on delineating the underlying brain structures and neural circuitry of these biases. The amygdala is engaged very early during threat exposure when discrete visual threats pass from the retina to the thalamus and immediately to the amygdala (Le Doux, 2000). It is thought these processes serve an adaptive function by providing quick albeit basic signals of threat to facilitate rapid detection and appropriate response (see Pine et al., 2008). As such, the amygdala is implicated early in threat attention orientation with rodent and human studies providing comparable evidence (Davis & Whalen, 2001). Therefore, one major implication of this cross-species process is that enhanced threat attention bias seen in anxiety is due to hypersensitivity in the amygdala.

A more gradual process involves the ventrolateral prefrontal cortex (vlPFC) which is thought to be implicated in emotion regulation and modulation of amygdala-based processes including threat attention bias (Monk et al., 2006; Monk et al., 2008; Phan, Fitzgerald, Nathan, & Tancer, 2006). In other words, greater activation of the vlPFC in anxious youths might be linked to greater effort required to down-regulate enhanced emotional reactivity stemming from amygdala activation (Pine et al., 2008).

Converging evidence also has accumulated implicating both the amygdala and the ventromedial regions of the prefrontal cortex (vmPFC) in memory circuits during fear extinction, the theoretical basis of exposure therapy in CBT (Quirk, Garcia, Gonzalez-Lima, 2006). As mentioned in the section on Traumatic and Stressful Life Events, associative models of fear conditioning emphasise the way in which an anxious reaction (fear) can become associated with a neutral stimulus (a dog) when it is paired with an aversive event (a bite) (see Boschen et al., 2009). During fear extinction (or exposure therapy), the feared stimulus (the dog) is repeatedly presented in the absence of the aversive event (a bite) until the anxious reaction subsides (fear). Thus, exposure therapy does not "extinguish" the original learning (dog – bite), but promotes new learning (dog – no bite). Whether fear returns in the future will depend on which fear memory is recalled, thereby implicating underlying neural circuits supporting fear memories.

Notably, research involving juvenile and adult rats suggests that whereas both the amygdala and the vmPFC are involved during extinction in adult rats, extinction in juvenile rats involves the amygdala but not the vmPFC (Kim & Richardson, 2010). As rodent and human circuitry share many similarities, this could suggest less cortical involvement underlying fear memories and new learning taking place during extinction (i.e., exposure therapy) in anxious children compared to anxious adults. Human studies of fear learning and extinction are few in number but emerging evidence suggests that anxious children are slower to extinguish fear responses (Waters, Henry, & Neumann, 2009).

HPA Axis Functioning

In stressful situations, the hypothalamus secretes corticotropin-releasing hormone (CRH), which stimulates the pituitary gland to secrete adrenocorticotrophic hormone (ACTH). Subsequently, ACTH is released which causes the adrenal glands to produce cortisol. Children with posttraumatic stress disorder show altered HPA axis functioning (Groenjian et al., 2003).

However, more recent studies found no differences in basal HPA axis functioning between distinct anxiety disorders in youth (Kallen et al., 2008). Instead, results indicated that basal HPA axis activity in childhood anxiety disorders is associated with anxiety scores on dimensional scales and not with the categorical DSM anxiety disorders. Anxious girls with higher anxiety showed lower morning rises in cortisol than anxious girls with lower anxiety, suggestive of hypo- instead of hyper-cortisolism (Gunnar & Vazquez, 2001). Also, higher separation anxiety scale scores and lower physical symptoms scale scores predicted higher cortisol at midday in anxious children, indicating that different aspects of anxiety are associated with cortisol levels in different ways (Kallen et al., 2008).

An Integrative Framework for Understanding the Causes and Maintenance of Childhood Anxiety Disorders

Assessment and treatment of childhood anxiety can be guided by the framework presented in Figure 1. The model highlights (a) the genetic and environmental risk factors for anxiety disorders and the influence they might have, both independently and collectively, on (b) underlying brain structures and circuitry which form the neural architecture underlying (c) observable psychological processes namely, threat attention bias, interpretation bias and impaired associative learning processes that characterise the expression of anxiety disorders and symptoms (d) (see Waters, Farrell et al., 2013 for detailed review).

At an individual case level, the model highlights the precise elements of a child's clinical presentation that require careful assessment, which in turn, forms the basis of case conceptualisation and treatment. As such, the emphasis placed upon key components of evidence-based treatments, such as cognitive-behavioural therapy (CBT), might vary from one child to the next.

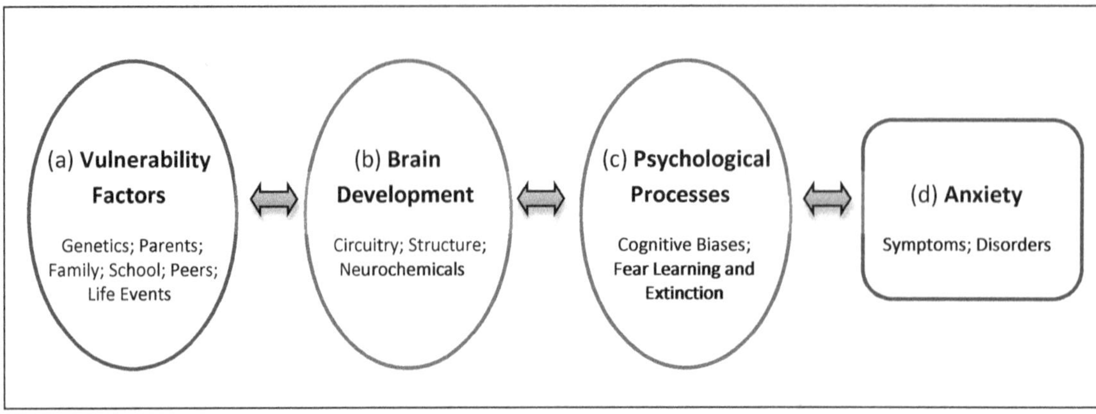

Figure 1 A framework for understanding the causal and maintaining factors involved in childhood anxiety.

Most CBT programs typically begin with psycho-education which describes links between sections (a) to (d) in Figure 1 above. Then more specific components of CBT interventions target the symptoms outlined in sections (c) and (d) through somatic management, cognitive restructuring, exposure therapy, and a combination of problem-solving skills, social skills training and other relapse prevention and maintenance strategies (e.g., Waters, Ford, Wharton, & Cobham, 2009). Many treatments also include parental involvement (a) (Cobham, Dadds, & Spence, 1998). Further information on how Take Action targets key components in this model is described in the next chapter *How to use this Practitioner Guide.*

References

Albano, A.M., Causey, D., & Carter, B. (2001). Fear and anxiety in children. In C.E. Waler & M. C. Roberts (Eds.), *Handbook of clinical child psychology* (3rd ed., 291–316). New York: Wiley.

Allen, J. L., Rapee, R. M., & Sandberg, S. (2008). Severe life events and chronic adversities as antecedents to anxiety in children: a matched control study. *Journal of Abnormal Child Psychology, 36*(7), 1047–1056. doi: 10.1007/s10802-008-9240-x

American Psychiatric Association. (2013). *Diagnostic and statistical manual of mental disorders (5th ed).* Washington, DC: American Psychiatric Association.

Anderson, J. C., Williams, S. M., McGee, R., & Silva, P. A. (1987). DSM-III disorders in preadolescent children: Prevalence in a large sample from the general population. *Archives of General Psychiatry, 44*, 69–76.

Andrews, G. (1996). Comorbidity in neurotic disorders: The similarities are more important than the differences. In R. M. Rapee (Ed.) *Current controversies in the anxiety disorders.* New York: The Guilford Press.

Bar-Haim, Y., Lamy, D., Pergamin, L., Bakermans-Kranenburg, M. J., & Van-Ijzendoorn, M. H. (2007). Threat-related attentional bias in anxious and non- anxious individuals: a meta-analytic study. *Psychological Bulletin, 133*, 1–24. doi: 10.1037/0033-2909.133.1.1

Barrett, P. M., Dadds, M. M., Rapee, R. M., & Ryan, S. M. (1996). Family enhancement of cognitive style in anxious and aggressive children. *Journal of Abnormal Child Psychology, 24*, 187–203.

Biederman, J., Faraone, S. V., Hirshfeld-Becker, D. R., Friedman, D., Robin, J. A., & Rosenbaum, J. F. (2001). Patterns of psychopathology and dysfunction in high-risk children of parents with panic disorder and major depression. *American Journal of Psychiatry, 158*, 49–57.

Biederman, J., Rosenbaum, J. F., Hirshfeld, D. R., Faraone, S. V., Bolduc, E. A., Gersten, M., . . . Reznick, S. (1990). Psychiatric correlates of behavioral inhibition in young children of parents with and without psychiatric disorders. *Archives of General Psychiatry, 47*(1), 21–26.

Bittner, A., Egger, H.L., Erkanli, A., Costello, J., Foley, D.L., & Angod, A. (2007). What do childhood anxiety disorders predict? *Journal of Child Psychology and Psychiatry, and Allied Disciplines 48*, 1174–1183.

Boschen, M. J., Neumann, D. L., & Waters, A. M. (2009). Relapse of successfully treated anxiety and fear: Theoretical issues and recommendations for clinical practice. *Australian and New Zealand Journal of Psychiatry*. *43*, 89–100.

Breton, J.-J., Bergeron, L., Valla, J.-P., Berthiaume, C., Gaudet, N., Lambert, J., St-Georges, M., Houde, L. and Lépine, S. (1999). Quebec Child Mental Health Survey: Prevalence of DSM-III-R Mental Health Disorders. *Journal of Child Psychology and Psychiatry*, *40*, 375–384. doi: 10.1111/1469-7610.00455.

Campbell, M. A. & Rapee, R. M. (1994). The nature of feared outcome representations in children. *Journal of Abnormal Child Psychology, 22*, 99–111.

Cartwright-Hatton, S., McNicol, K., & Doubleday, E. (2006). Anxiety in a neglected population: Prevalence of anxiety disorders in pre-adolescent children. *Clinical Psychology Review, 26*, 817–833. doi.org/10.1016/j.cpr.2005.12.002.

Chorpita, B. F., & Barlow, D. H. (1998). The development of anxiety: The role of control in the early environment. *Psychological Bulletin, 124*(1), 3–21.

Cobham, V. E., Dadds, M. R., & Spence, S. H. (1998). The role of parental anxiety in the treatment of childhood anxiety. *Journal of Consulting and Clinical Psychology*, 66, 893–905.

Connell, A. M., & Goodman, S. H. (2002). The association between psychopathology in fathers versus mothers and children's internalizing and externalizing behavior problems: A meta-analysis. *Psychological Bulletin, 128*, 746 – 773.

Colletti, C. J. M., Forehand, R., Garai, E., Rakow, A., McKee, L., Fear, J. M., & Compas, B. E. (2009). Parent depression and child anxiety: An overview of the literature and clinical implications. *Child Youth Care Forum*, 38, 151–160.

Costello, E.J., Egger, H.L., & Angold, A. (2004). The developmental epidemiology of anxiety disorders. In T. Ollendick, & J. March (Eds.), *Phobic and anxiety disorders in children and adolescents: a clinician's guide to effective psychosocial and pharmacological interventions* (pp. 61–91). New York: Oxford University Press.

Craske, M. G. (2003). *Origins of phobias and anxiety disorders: Why more women than men?* Oxford: Elsevier.

Craske, M. G., & Waters, A. M. (2005). Panic disorder, phobias, and generalized anxiety disorder. *Annual Review of Clinical Psychology, 1*, 197–225.

Creswell, C., Schniering, C. A., & Rapee, R. M. (2005). Threat interpretation in anxious children and their mothers: Comparison with non-clinical children and the effects of treatment. *Behaviour Research and Therapy*, *43*, 1375–1381.

Curry, J. F., March, J.S., & Hervey, A.S. (2004). Comorbidity of childhood and adolescent anxiety disorders. In T. H. Ollendick & J. S. Marsh (Eds.), *Phobic and anxiety disorders in children and adolescents* (pp. 116–140). New York: Oxford University Press.

Davis, M., & Whalen, P.J. (2001). The amygdala: Vigilance and emotion. *Molecular Psychiatry*, 6, 13–34.

DiBartolo, P. M., & Helt, M. (2007). Theoretical models of affectionate versus affectionless control in anxious families: a critical examination based on observations of parent-child interactions. *Clinical Child and Family Psychology Review*, *10*(3), 253–274. doi: 10.1007/s10567-007-0017-5

Eley, T. C., & Stevenson, J. (2000). Specific life events and chronic experiences differentially associated with depression and anxiety in young twins. *Journal Abnormal Child Psychology*, *28*(4), 383–394.

Field, A. P. & Cartwright-Hatton, S. (2008). Shared and unique cognitive factors in social anxiety. *International Journal of Cognitive Therapy*, *1*, 206–222.

Ford, T., Goodman, R., & Meltzer, H. (2003). The British child and adolescent mental health survey 1999: The prevalence of DSM-IV disorders. *Journal of the American Academy of Child and Adolescent Psychiatry*, *42*, 1203–1211.

Gerull, F. C., & Rapee, R. M. (2002). Mother knows best: effects of maternal modelling on the acquisition of fear and avoidance behaviour in toddlers. *Behaviour Research and Therapy*, *40*(3), 279–287.

Ginsburg, G. S., Grover, R. L., & Ialongo, N. (2004). Parenting Behaviors Among Anxious and Non-Anxious Mothers: Relation with Concurrent and Long-Term Child Outcomes. *Child & Family Behavior Therapy*, *26*, 23–41.

Ginsburg, G. S., La Greca, A. M., & Silverman, W. K. (1998). Social anxiety in children with anxiety disorders: Relation with social and emotional functioning. *Journal of Abnormal Child Psychology*, *26*, 175–185.

Goodyer, I. M., & Altham, P. M. (1991). Lifetime exit events and recent social and family adversities in anxious and depressed school-age children and adolescents—II. *Journal of Affective Disorders*, *21*(4), 229–238.

Goenjian, A. K., Pynoos, R. S., Steinberg, A. M., Endres, D., Abraham, K., Geffner, M. E., & Fairbanks, L. A. (2003). Hypothalamic-pituitary-adrenal activity among Armenian adolescents with PTSD symptoms. *Journal of Traumatic Stress*, *16*, 319–323.

Gunnar, M. R, & Vazquez, D. M. (2001). Low cortisol and a flattening of expected daytime rhythm: potential indices of risk in human development. *Developmental Psychopathology*, *13*, 515–538.

Hettema, J. M., Neale, M. C., & Kendler, K. S. (2001). A Review and Meta-Analysis of the Genetic Epidemiology of Anxiety Disorders. *American Journal of Psychiatry*, *158*, 1568–1578.

Hirshfeld-Becker, D. R., Biederman, J., Henin, A., Faraone, S. V., Davis, S., Harrington, K., & Rosenbaum, J. F. (2007). Behavioral inhibition in preschool children at risk is a specific predictor of middle childhood social anxiety: a five-year follow-up. *Journal of Developmental and Behavioral Pediatrics*, 28(3), 225–233. doi: 10.1097/01.DBP.0000268559.34463.d0

Hudson, J.L., Gradisar, M., Gamble, A., Schniering, C., & Rebelo, I. (2009). The sleep patterns and problems of clinically anxious children. *Behaviour Research and Therapy*, 47, 339–344.

Hudson, J. L., & Rapee, R. M. (2009). Familial and social environments in the etiology and maintenance of anxiety disorders. In M. M. Antony, & M. B. Stein (Eds.) *Oxford handbook of anxiety and related disorders* (pp. 173–189). New York: Oxford University Press.

Hudson, J. L., Doyle, A. M., & Gar, N. (2009). Child and maternal influence on parenting behavior in anxious children. *Journal of Clinical Child and Adolescent Psychology, 38(2)*, 256–262.

Kagan, J., Reznick, J. S., Snidman, N., Gibbons, J., & Johnson, M. O. (1988). Childhood Derivatives of Inhibition and Lack of Inhibition to the Unfamiliar. *Child Development*, 59(6), 1580–1589. doi: DOI 10.1111/j.1467-8624.1988.tb03685.x

Kagan, J., Snidman, N., Kahn, V., & Towsley, S. (2007). The preservation of two infant temperaments into adolescence. *Monographs of the Society for Research in Child Development*, *72*(2), 1–75, vii; discussion 76–91. doi: 10.1111/j.1540-5834.2007.00436.x

Kagan, J., & Snidman, N. (1999). Early childhood predictors of adult anxiety disorders. *Biological Psychiatry*, *46*(11), 1536–1541.

Kallen, V. L., Tulen, J. H. M., Utens, E., et al. (2008). Associations between HPA axis functioning and level of anxiety in children and adolescents with an anxiety disorder. *Depression and Anxiety*, *25*, 131–141.

Kashani, J. H., & Orvaschel, H. (1990). A community study of anxiety in children and adolescents. *American Journal of Psychiatry*, *147*, 313–318.

Kendall, P. C., & Ollendick, T. H. (2004). Setting the research and practice agenda for anxiety in children and adolescence: A topic comes of age. *Cognitive and Behavioral Practice*, *11*, 65–74.

Kessler, R. C., Foster, C. L., Saunders, W. B., & Stang, P. E. (1995). Social consequences of psychiatric disorders, I: Educational attainment. *American Journal of Psychiatry*, *152*, 1026–1032.

Kessler, R. C., Berglund, P., Demler, O., Jin, R., Merikangas, K. R., & Walters, E. E. (2005). Lifetime prevalence and age-of-onset distributions of DSM-IV disorders in the National Comorbidity Survey Replication. *Archives of General Psychiatry*, 62, 593–602.

Kim, J. H., & Richardson, R. (2010). New Findings on Extinction of Conditioned Fear Early in Development: Theoretical and Clinical Implications. *Biological Psychiatry*, *67*, 297–303. doi: 10.1016/j.biopsych.2009.09.003.

King, N. J., Ollier, K., Iacuone, R., Schuster, S., Bays, K., Gullone, E., & Ollendick, T. H. (1989). Fears of children and adolescents: A cross-sectional Australian study using the Revised-Fear Survey Schedule for children. *Journal of Child Psychology and Psychiatry and Allied Disciplines*, *30*, 775–784.

Last, C. G., Strauss, C. C., & Francis, G. (1987). Comorbidity among childhood anxiety disorders. *Journal of Nervous & Mental Disorders*, *175*, 726–730.

Le Doux, J. E. (2000). Emotion circuits in the brain. *Annual Review of Neuroscience*, *23*, 155–184.

Masi, G., Favilla, L., Millepiedi, S., & Mucci, M. (2000). Somatic symptoms in children and adolescents referred for emotional and behavioural disorders. *Psychiatry*, *63*, 140–149.

McLeod, B. D., Wood, J. J., & Weisz, J. R. (2007). Examining the association between parenting and childhood anxiety: a meta-analysis. *Clinical Psychology Review*, *27*(2), 155–172. doi: 10.1016/j.cpr.2006.09.002.

Mogg, K. & Bradley, B. P. (1998). A cognitive-motivational analysis of anxiety. *Behaviour Research and Therapy*, *36*(9), 809–848.

Monk, C. S., Nelson, E. E., McClure, E. B., Mogg, K., Bradley, B. P., et al. (2006). Ventrolateral prefrontal cortex activation and attentional bias in response to angry faces in adolescents with generalized anxiety disorder. *The American Journal of Psychiatry*, *163*, 1091–1097.

Monk, C. S., Telzer, E. H., Mogg, K., Bradley, B. P., Mai, X., et al. (2008). Amygdala and ventrolateral prefrontal cortex activation to masked angry faces in children and adolescents with generalized anxiety disorder. *Archives of General Psychiatry, 65*, 568–576.

Moore, P. S., Whaley, S. E., & Sigman, M. (2004). Interactions between mothers and children: impacts of maternal and child anxiety. *Journal of Abnormal Psychology, 113*(3), 471–476. doi: 10.1037/0021-843X.113.3.471

Muris, P., Merckelbach, H., & Collaris, R. (1997). Common childhood fears and their origins. *Behaviour Research and Therapy, 35*, 929–937.

Muris, P., van Brakel, A. M., Arntz, A., & Schouten, E. (2011). Behavioral inhibition as a risk factor for the development of childhood anxiety disorders: A longitudinal study. *Journal of Child and Family Studies, 20*, 157–170.

Murray, L., Creswell, C., & Cooper, P. J. (2009). The development of anxiety disorders in childhood: an integrative review. *Psychological Medicine, 39*, 1413–1423.

Niles, A. N., Mesri, B., Burklund, L. J., Lieberman, M. D., & Craske, M. G. (2013). Attentional bias and emotional reactivity as predictors and moderators of behavioral treatment for social phobia. Behaviour Research and Therapy, *51*, 669–679.

Perez-Edgar, K., & Fox, N. A. (2005). Temperament and Anxiety Disorders. *Child and Adolescent Psychiatric Clinics of North America, 14*, 681–706.

Perez-Edgar, K., Roberson-Nay, R., Hardin, M. G., Poeth, K., Guyer, A. E., et al. (2007) Attention alters neural responses to evocative faces in behaviorally inhibited adolescents. *Neuroimage, 35*, 1538–1546.

Phan, K. L., Fitzgerald, D. A., Nathan, P. J., & Tancer, M. E. (2006) Association between amygdale hyperactivity to harsh faces and severity of social anxiety in generalized social phobia. *Biological Psychiatry, 59*, 424–429.

Pine, D. S., Guyer, A. E., & Leibenluft, E. (2008). Functional magnetic resonance imaging and pediatric anxiety. *Journal of American Academy of Child & Adolescent Psychiatry, 47*, 1217–1221.

Price, M., Tone, E. B., & Anderson, P. L. (2011). Vigilant and avoidant attention biases as predictors of response to cognitive behavioural therapy for social phobia. *Depression & Anxiety, 28*, 349–353. doi: 10.1002/da.20791

Prior, M., Smart, D., Sanson, A., & Oberklaid, F. (2000). Does shy-inhibited temperament in childhood lead to anxiety problems in adolescence? *Journal of the American Academy of Child and Adolescent Psychiatry, 39*(4), 461–468. doi: 10.1097/00004583-200004000-00015.

Quirk, G. J., Garcia, R., & Gonzalez-Lima, F. (2006). Prefrontal mechanisms in extinction of conditioned fear. *Biological Psychiatry, 60*, 337–343.

Rapee, R. M. (1997). Potential role of childrearing practices in the development of anxiety and depression. *Clinical Psychology Review, 17*, 47–67.

Rapee, R. M. (2001). The development of generalized anxiety. In M. W. Vasey & M. R. Dadds (Eds.), *The Developmental Psychopathology of Anxiety* (pp. 481–503). New York: Oxford University Press.

Rapee, R. M. (2002). The development and modification of temperamental risk for anxiety disorders: Prevention of a lifetime of anxiety? *Biological Psychiatry, 52*, 947–957.

Rapee, R. M., Schniering, C. A., & Hudson, J. L. (2009). Anxiety disorders during childhood and adolescence: Origins and treatment. *Annual Review of Clinical Psychology, 5*, 311–341.

Rose, A. J., & Rudolph, K. D. (2006). A review of sex differences in peer relationship processes: Potential trade-offs for the emotional and behavioural development of girls and boys. *Psychological Bulletin, 132*, 98–131.

Salum, G. A., K, M., Bradley, B. P., Gadelha, A., Pan, P., R., Tamanaha, A. C., . . . Pine, D. S. (2013). Threat bias in attention orienting: evidence of specificity in a large community-based study. *Psychological Medicine, 43*, 733–745.

Spence, S. H., Donovan, C., Brechman-Toussaint, M. (1999). Social skills, social outcomes, and cognitive features of childhood social phobia. *Journal of Abnormal Psychology*. *108*, 211–221. doi: 10.1037/0021-843X.108.2.211.

Strauss, C. C., Lahey, B. B., Frick, P., Frame, C. L., & Hynd, G. W. (1988). Peer social status of children with anxiety disorders. *Journal of Consulting and Clinical Psychology*. 56, 137–141. doi: 10.1037/0022-006X.56.1.137.

Torgensen, S. (1983). Genetic factors in anxiety disorders. *Archives of General Psychiatry, 40, 1085–1089*.

Velez, C. N., Johnson, J., & Cohen, P. (1989). A longitudinal analysis of selected risk factors for childhood psychopathology. *Journal of the American Academy of Child and Adolescent Psychiatry, 28*, 861–864.

Verduin, T. L., & Kendall, P. C. (2008). Peer perceptions and liking of children with anxiety disorders. *Journal of Abnormal Child Psychology*, 36, 459–469. doi: 10.1007/s10802-007-9192-6.

Waters, A. M., Craske, M. G., Bergman, R. L., & Treanor, M. (2008). Threat interpretation bias as a vulnerability factor in childhood anxiety disorders. *Behaviour Research and Therapy*, 46, 39–47.

Waters, A. M., Wharton, T. A., Zimmer-Gembeck, M. J., & Craske, M. G. (2008). Threat-based cognitive biases in anxious children: Comparison with non-anxious children before and after cognitive-behavioural treatment. *Behaviour Research and Therapy*, 46, 358–374.

Waters, A. M., Henry, J., & Neumann, D. L. (2009). Aversive Pavlovian conditioning in childhood anxiety disorders: Impaired response inhibition and resistance to extinction. *Journal of Abnormal Psychology*, *118*, 311–321.

Waters, A. M., Mogg, K., & Bradley, B. P. (2012). The direction of threat attention bias predicts treatment outcome from cognitive behavioural therapy in anxious children. *Behaviour Research and Therapy*, 50, 428–434.

Waters, A. M., Farrell, L. J., & Schilpzand, E. (2013). Neuropsychological assessment and clinical intervention for youth with anxiety disorders. In L.A. Reddy, A.Weissman., & J.B., Hale (Eds.), *Neuropsychological assessment and intervention for youth: An evidence-based approach to emotional and behavioral disorders* (pp. 13–40). Washington DC: American Psychological Association Press.

Waters, A. M., Schilpzand, E., Bell, C., Walker, L. S., & Barber, K. (2013). Functional gastrointestinal symptoms in anxious children. *Journal of Abnormal Child Psychology, 41*, 151–163.

Waters, A. M., Bradley, B. P., & Mogg, K. (2014). Biased attention to threat in paediatric anxiety disorders (generalized anxiety disorder, social phobia, specific phobia, separation anxiety disorder) as a function of 'distress' versus 'fear' diagnostic categorization. *Psychological Medicine*. 44, 607–616.

Weissman, M. M., Wickramaratne, P., Nomura, Y., Warner, Y., Pilowsky, D., & Verdeli, H. (2006). Offspring of Depressed Parents: 20 years later. *American Journal of Psychiatry*, *163*, 1001–1008.

Whaley S. E., Pinto, A., & Sigman, M. (1999). Characterizing interactions between anxious mothers and their children. *Journal of Consulting and Clinical Psychology*, 67, 826–836.

Williams, J. M. G., Watts, F. N., Macleod, C., & Mathews, A. (1997). *Cognitive psychology and emotional disorders* (2nd ed.). Chichester: Wiley

Wood, J. J., McLeod, B. D., Sigman, M., Hwang, W. C., & Chu, B. C. (2003). Parenting and childhood anxiety: theory, empirical findings, and future directions. *Journal of child psychology and psychiatry, and allied disciplines*, *44*, 134–151.

How to use this Practitioner Guide

Organisation of this Guide

Following this chapter are seven practitioner modules, which use a standardised layout of content, to guide you through the steps covered in each module. The first module is designed specifically for practitioners who wish to include an assessment phase before and/or after treatment with a child or group of children. Six treatment modules follow the assessment module. The first treatment module has two parts — 1.1 contains extra instructions for running a Take Action group. It can be skipped when working with an individual child. The six treatment modules can be used sequentially across ten weeks to provide an individual or group treatment protocol or used as stand-alone guides to teach specific skills.

The layout of each module includes specific sections that will help orient the practitioner to the key principles of the Take Action program. These are described below.

Major Activities in this Module

Provides an agenda of the topics and major activities to be completed for each module in the program. The relevant handouts for each activity are listed under each activity. Each handout is labelled by *module name*, followed by who it is for (i.e. *child* or *parent*), followed by the handout *number* within that module (e.g., *BeAware-child-1*). All the child and parent handouts across all modules are provided in the Appendices of this Guidebook.

Activity Description

Provides information about the goals of each activity. It is recommended that the practitioner follows the instructions provided for each activity closely to ensure that the treatment techniques are taught consistently.

For Children

Specific instructions are provided for each activity to complete with children and the relevant handouts are explained.

For Parents

Specific instructions are provided for each activity to complete with parents and the relevant handouts are explained.

Following the assessment and treatment modules are two chapters covering important issues to be considered when using the Take Action program. The first features information and support when working with children who have comorbid conditions and the second is a trouble shooting guide.

Aims of Take Action

Take Action was developed to assist boys and girls between four and 12 years of age. The program aims to teach children helpful ways to cope with and manage anxiety (e.g., Waters, Wharton, Zimmer-Gembeck, & Craske, 2008; Waters, Ford, Wharton, & Cobham, 2009). The program has been used with children diagnosed with generalised anxiety disorder, separation anxiety disorder, social phobia and specific phobias. The word ACTION is a coping-oriented acronym used throughout the program. Children are encouraged to *take action* against their anxiety. This means children approach their fears and worries using the well-researched and effective strategies learnt during the program.

A growing body of evidence indicates that anxiety disorders in childhood can be successfully treated with Cognitive Behavioural Therapy (CBT) interventions (James, Soler & Weatherall, 2007). CBT programs address the physiological (e.g. somatic symptoms), cognitive (e.g. negative, threat-related thoughts), and behavioural processes (e.g. avoidance) which are thought to cause and maintain anxiety in children. CBT enables children to identify their anxiety and to apply skills to gradually approach anxiety-provoking situations.

CBT programs generally include:

- Psycho-education about anxiety.
- Somatic management of physiological symptoms.
- Cognitive restructuring (i.e., developing realistic expectations and coping self-talk).
- Graded exposure to anxiety-provoking situations.
- Problem solving skills.
- Social skills training (e.g. assertiveness).
- Relapse prevention and maintenance of skills.

Take Action includes the above CBT components and also integrates treatment techniques derived from recent advances in our understanding of the threat-based cognitive biases and maladaptive thinking styles that characterise anxiety disorders.

During the program, parents are encouraged to positively reinforce their child for successful handling of his or her anxious/avoidant behaviours. In addition, the program aims to improve parenting skills and the parent–child relationship.

Anxiety Disorders Covered by Take Action

Generalised Anxiety Disorder (GAD)

GAD was previously referred to as over-anxious disorder (American Psychiatric Association [APA], 2000) and is characterised by excessive or unrealistic worry or anxiety over a range of life areas. Children typically worry about future events, past behaviour, academic or athletic achievement and social interactions. They often engage in excessive reassurance seeking, are often perfectionistic and highly conscientious (Dadds, Heard & Rapee, 1991). A number of somatic complaints are reported including sleep disturbance, fatigue, general tension and inability to relax.

Separation Anxiety Disorder (SAD)

SAD is an unrealistic fear of separation from a major attachment figure (i.e., mother / father). Children with SAD become extremely distressed and frightened whenever they become separated from their attachment figures and engage in many behaviours aimed at avoiding such a possibility (Dadds et al., 1991; Silverman & Ginsburg, 1995). Children with SAD may have difficulty attending school. In addition to behavioural manifestations, children with SAD also engage in considerable worry, such as concerns over the possibility of being kidnapped, accidents or death, either to themselves or their attachment figure. Children with SAD report a number of physical complaints such as headaches, stomach aches or general sickness, especially upon impending separation.

Social Phobia

Social phobia (or social anxiety disorder) is characterised by a persistent fear and/or avoidance of social situations in which the person is exposed to unfamiliar persons or to potential social evaluation and scrutiny (APA, 2000). Social anxiety can affect individuals across the developmental spectrum. Early onset of social phobia may be particularly impairing because of its disruptive effects on social and academic functioning during a child's formative years. Thus it appears that the ability to recognise and monitor or remediate social anxiety early in development may be of great advantage in reversing its potentially debilitating course (Morris, Hirshfeld-Becker, Henin & Storch, 2004).

Specific Phobia

Specific fears are highly prevalent in childhood (Gullone, 2000), yet most of them are short-lived and dissipate within months (Muris, Verweij & Meesters, 2003). However, in some children, specific fears persist and interfere with normal functioning, warranting a diagnosis of specific phobia (APA, 2000; Muris, Merckelbach, Mayer & Prins, 2000). The essential feature of specific phobia is a persistent and irrational fear of a specific object, activity or situation (the phobic stimulus) that results in an active avoidance of that specific object, activity or situation. In children some of the common types of specific phobia are fears of animals, blood-injury situations, storms, and darkness (Muris et al., 2003; Ollendick, King, & Muris, 2002).

Other Anxiety Disorders

Children experiencing OCD, panic disorder and/or post-traumatic stress disorder have not been included in treatment studies using this program. It should be noted that some studies have included children with these diagnoses in group-based CBT programs (e.g., Rapee, Abbott, & Lyneham, 2006), while others have adopted a disorder-specific treatment approach (e.g., Farrell, Waters, Milliner, & Ollendick, 2012; Pincus, May Whitton, Mattis, & Barlow, 2010; see Curry & Murphy, 1995; and Silverman et al., 2008 for reviews).

Children are taught a range of CBT strategies during the program via a 6- step ACTION plan. Each letter in the word ACTION stands for a skill children learn:

A Be AWARE - The first step in the ACTION plan teaches children to be AWARE of their feelings and learn to recognise when they feel anxious. Children will also learn to be AWARE of signals in their bodies that indicate they are feeling anxious.

C Keep CALM - Once children learn to be AWARE of signs of anxiety, the second step in the ACTION plan teaches children strategies to keep CALM and reduce their anxiety. These strategies include On The Spot Deep Breathing and Move My Muscles Relaxation.

T THINK Strong Thoughts - Building on from being AWARE and keeping CALM, the third step in the ACTION plan teaches children to THINK positively and confidently. Children learn strategies for turning Scared (unhelpful) thoughts into Strong (positive) thoughts.

I Get INTO ACTION - The fourth step in the ACTION plan encourages children to gradually confront anxiety-provoking situations using an ACTION Ladder (a step-by-step graded exposure hierarchy). Children practise the Be AWARE, Keep CALM and THINK Strong Thoughts steps while climbing their ACTION Ladder/s. Children are encouraged to reward themselves for taking ACTION against their anxiety.

O Use my OPTIONS - The fifth step in the ACTION plan teaches children additional strategies (or OPTIONS) to further manage their anxiety including problem solving, asking supportive others for help, and focusing on the positives. Children are also taught social skills (e.g., confident body signals, assertiveness, dealing with bullying strategies) to further enhance their coping abilities.

N NEVER stop taking ACTION - The last step in the ACTION plan encourages children to plan for anxiety-provoking times so they can keep taking ACTION against anxiety in the future.

Figure 2 What does the ACTION in Take Action stand for?

Age Appropriateness for Take Action

The program is applicable for children between four and 12 years of age. It is often best to separate children into two age brackets when running the program in the group format with a range of ages: 4–7 year olds and 8–12 year olds. The term **'children'** is used throughout this guide to refer to children aged four to 12 years. However, if anything specific to 4–7 year old children is discussed the term **'younger children'** is used. At times the practitioner may need to match the handout instructions to the child's developmental level and/or read the content of each handout to the child. Younger children may also need their parents to write out their answers for them on the handouts. Younger children can be asked to draw certain concepts throughout the program if this is easier for the child than writing down their answers. However, the handouts are designed to contain detailed information so that children can look back at these resources in years to come and follow the key strategies covered during the program.

What does the ACTION in Take Action stand for?

Children are taught a range of CBT strategies during the program via a six step ACTION plan. Each letter in the word ACTION stands for a skill children learn (see Figure 2 opposite).

How Take Action Works with the 3-Response-System of Anxiety

The theoretical model for the treatment of anxiety addresses physiological, cognitive and behavioural responses. Figure 3 on page 23 shows the physiological, cognitive and behavioural responses associated with anxiety, and how each of the responses is addressed through the steps in the ACTION plan.

Introducing the Sea Animals

Take Action was developed in Australia which has a strong beach culture. A majority of the population live close to the sea and are familiar with marine life. A variety of sea animals are included in the program to assist children's understanding of the anxiety management strategies taught. Dulcy and Dion the dolphins are the central sea animal characters used in the program.

The other sea animals below are used to assist children to understand their emotions better: Clare the clam, Shawn the shark, Wendy the whale, and Tommy the turtle.

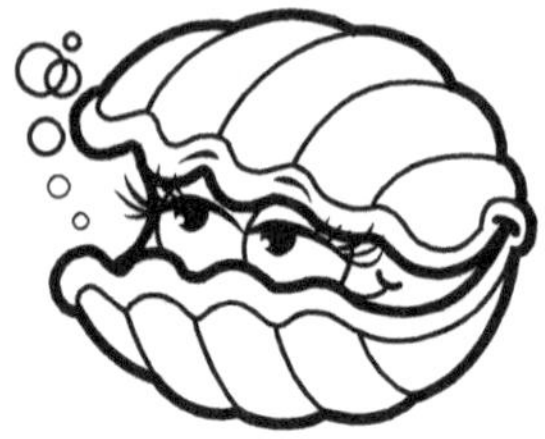

Using Take Action with Groups and Individuals

Children can participate in Take Action within either a small group or individual therapy environment. They should attend 10 sessions with each session running for approximately 60 minutes (see below for adaptations to this approach for schools). Children are provided with their own copy of the *Take Action Child Handout Workbook* (purchased separately) so they can practise their strategies at home. Table 1 on page 24 illustrates the 10-session design.

It is most beneficial for children to attend group or individual therapy on a weekly basis until the ACTION plan is learnt. However, there may be obstacles to attending weekly sessions, such as the family's ability to attend such frequent sessions, the cost, number of sessions allowed under any public or private medical benefits scheme, or the practitioner's availability. In these situations, it is important that the child and parents attend sessions as regularly as possible in order to maximise the likelihood of anxiety levels reducing.

When running the program in the group environment, it is recommended that no more than 6–8 children participate at one time in the 8–12 year old age group; and

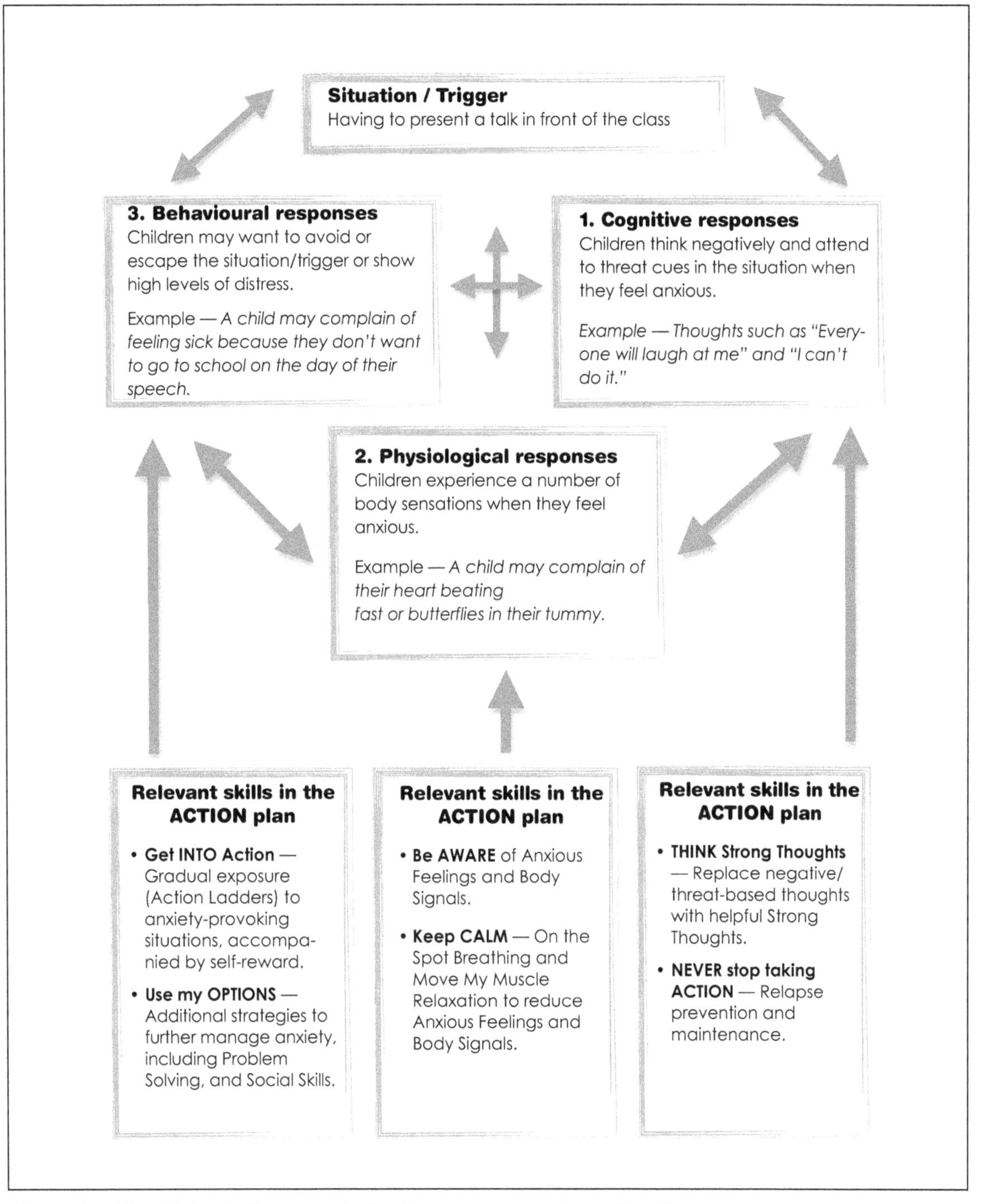

Figure 3 How Take Action targets the 3-response-system of anxiety

no more than 6 children participate in the 4–7 year age group. It is important that each group member is encouraged to play an active role in the group learning process. The group room needs to be large enough, and with adequate floor space, for all activities to be conducted in comfort. The group room should be free from interruption, noise and other distractions. It is helpful to have children sit on chairs around a table, or on soft cushions around a low table if sitting on the floor. Chairs for parent sessions

Table 1 10-session Take Action design.

Take Action Module	Session Number	Child Content	Session Number	Parent Content
Be AWARE	1	Introduction to a Take ACTION Group	1	Introduction to Take ACTION
Be AWARE	2	Recognising signs of anxiety	2	Instruction about the Be AWARE and Keep CALM steps
Keep CALM	3	Learning relaxation techniques		-
THINK Strong Thoughts	4–5	Learning to THINK positive, ACTION-oriented thoughts	3	Instruction about the THINK Strong Thoughts step Parent Management strategies
Get INTO Action	6	Learning to approach anxiety-provoking situations	4	Instruction about the Get INTO ACTION step
Use my OPTIONS	7	Learning additional coping strategies	5	Instruction about the Use my OPTIONS and NEVER stop taking ACTION steps
NEVER stop taking ACTION	8–10	Learning to use all the steps in the ACTION plan for the future	6	Instruction about the NEVER stop taking ACTION step

may be arranged in a semi-circle to encourage discussion. All the child and parent handouts across all modules are provided as photocopiable masters in the Appendices of this Guidebook or can be purchased separately as bound booklets (see *www.take-actionprogram.com* for further information).

Using Take Action in Schools

With minor adaptations Take Action has been used successfully in schools, either on an individual basis or with small groups of children identified by guidance counsellors and teachers, and it has also been delivered classroom-wide (e.g., Waters, Groth, Sanders, O'Brien, & Zimmer-Gembeck, 2015). In all cases, the Take Action program has been delivered by registered psychologists or school guidance counsellors. To date, Take Action has not been delivered in schools by teachers, learning support staff, school nurses, or other school staff. Indeed, there is mixed evidence regarding whether classroom-based CBT delivered by trained teachers and other school staff is as effective as classroom-based CBT delivered by trained psychologists and other health facilitators (Barrett & Turner, 2001; Stallard et al., 2014). In the cases where the Take Action program has been delivered classroom-wide in schools, it has been modified to be delivered once per week over 8 to 10 weeks to fit within the school term and co-facilitated by registered psychologists.

Parent Involvement in Take Action

Parent involvement is considered important in the program to help consolidate learning and reinforce children's efforts to confront their fears between sessions. Parents are introduced to each step of the ACTION plan in parallel with the information children are learning (see Table 1 on previous page). In addition, parents learn positive parenting strategies that will assist their child in taking ACTION against anxiety. Six Parent Information Sessions are used to encourage parents to become actively involved in their child's learning and therapeutic process. Running the parent sessions as a separate group program to the children's group sessions creates a supportive environment that fosters an understanding of children's difficulties and sharing of parental experiences. In the individual therapy environment, it is important that the parent/s spend adequate time with the practitioner to understand the information and how it applies to their child.

It is recommended that booster (follow-up) sessions for children and their parents are conducted after completion of the program. The booster sessions are used to encourage children and parents to review their progress, problem solve, and reinforce the CBT strategies learnt in the program. The frequency of these booster sessions is based on the child and family's needs. As a guide, the authors of Take Action usually complete booster sessions at one month, three months, and six months intervals.

Practitioner Skills Required for Take Action

In writing this Guide, the authors have assumed that the practitioner has sound microskills, interpersonal abilities and experience working with children and families. However, we briefly mention the following skills that we see as paramount to working with anxious children and their parents.

In the early stages of the program, the practitioner focuses on developing a strong therapeutic alliance with the child and their family. The practitioner should actively involve children and parents by encouraging participation in activities, and fostering a sense of confidence that they can *take action* against their anxiety. The concept of being on the child's "Strong Team" is discussed with parents in their first session. It is very important that the child and family feel they are collaborating with the practitioner, and they are all working on the same strong team. The practitioner aims to engage the child in the therapy process by promoting a positive, friendly atmosphere. Discussion about the child's interests and hobbies is important during this phase. It also allows the practitioner to gather relevant child and family examples that can be used later in the treatment program.

Empathy and support should be given at all times throughout the sessions. This will help children and parents to feel supported, encouraged and understood, and also assist the rapport building process. This includes both non-verbal reinforcement (i.e., smile, nod, eye contact) and verbal reinforcement (i.e., praise for participation, such as *You participated really well in that last activity*). Children and parents should be given specific feedback about their progress and participation. In particular, the practitioner should review the Home Tasks at the beginning of each session, and children should be congratulated for completing the activities outside of session. The practitioner can also assist the child to problem-solve and overcome any obstacles. The practitioner uses psycho-education and the hypothetical situations described in the program to assist the child's understanding of the Take Action concepts. Other relevant examples can be used from the child's life when necessary to further engage the child in discussion. The practitioner models each of the new concepts as the program progresses. There is a strong role playing component involved in the social skills part of the program. In a group setting, these role plays assist children to complete real-life practise of the skills with same-aged peers. When working individually with children, siblings can be invited into these social skills sessions to assist with the role plays.

Practitioner Checklist

It is recommended that the practitioner follows each step of the checklist below to ensure the Take Action program is run as effectively as possible. Read carefully through each step and tick it off when the task has been completed.

___ **Step 1.** (IMPORTANT) Read the Introduction and chapter on the Causes and Maintenance of childhood anxiety disorders, so you develop a thorough understanding of the factors that could be causing and maintaining anxiety in children you work with.

___ **Step 2.** Read this section (How to use this Practitioner Guide) thoroughly to ensure you are familiar with the aims of the program. It is vital that the practitioner understands the key principles behind each step of the ACTION plan, and how to implement the activities with children and parents, either in the individual or group therapy environments.

___ **Step 3.** Based on your assessment of the child and his/her parents, choose your program format:

________________ (4–7 years old; 8–12 years old)

________________ (Individual; group therapy)

___ **Step 4.** Familiarise yourself with the handouts.

___ **Step 5.** Ensure each child and parent/s at the beginning of each session has their own copy of all handouts or their own handout booklets (*Take Action Child Handout Workbook, Take Action Parent Handout Workbook).*

The handout, *BeAware-child-2B*, which summarises the six steps in the ACTION plan should be kept handy so the practitioner can frequently refer to it throughout the program. It is helpful to use this handout each session so that children and parents know which step they are up to in the ACTION Plan.

References

American Psychiatric Association. (2000). *Diagnostic and statistical manual of mental disorders* (4th ed., Text Revision). Washington, DC: Author.

Barrett, P. M., & Turner, C. (2001). Prevention of anxiety symptoms in primary school children: Preliminary results from a universal school-based trial. *British Journal of Clinical Psychology*, *40*, 399–410.

Curry, J. F., & Murphy, L. B. (1995). Comorbidity of anxiety disorders. In J. S. March (Ed.), *Anxiety disorders in children and adolescents* (pp. 301–317). New York: The Guilford Press.

Dadds, M. R., Heard, P. M., & Rapee, R. M. (1991). Anxiety disorders in children. *International Review of Psychiatry*, *3*, 231–241.

Farrell, L. J., Waters, A. M., Milliner, E., & Ollendick, T. (2012). Comorbidity and treatment response in paediatric OCD: Outcomes of group cognitive behavioural therapy. *Psychiatry Research*, *199*, 115–123.

Gullone, E. (2000). The development of normal fear: A century of research. *Clinical Psychology Review*, *20* (4), 429–451.

James, A., Soler, A., & Weatherall, R. (2007). Cochrane review: Cognitive behavioural therapy for anxiety disorders in children and adolescents. *Evidence-Based Child Health: A Cochrane Review Journal*, *2* (4), 1248–1275.

Morris, T. L., Hirshfeld-Becker, D. R., Henin, A., & Storch, E. A. (2004). Developmentally sensitive assessment of social anxiety. *Cognitive and Behavioural Practice*, *11*, 13–28.

Muris, P., Merckelbach, H., Mayer, B., & Prins, E. (2000). How serious are common childhood fears? *Behaviour Research and Therapy*, *38*, 217–228.

Muris, P., Verweij, C., & Meesters, C. (2003). The "anti-monster letter" as a simple therapeutic tool for reducing night-time fears in young children. *Behaviour Change*, *20* (4), 200–207.

Ollendick, T. H., King, N. J., & Muris, P. (2002). Fears and phobias in children: Phenomenology, epidemiology and aetiology, *Child and Adolescent Mental Health*, *7*, 98–106.

Pincus, D. B., May, J., Whitton, S. W., Mattis, S. G., & Barlow, D. H. (2010). Cognitive-behavioral treatment of panic disorder in adolescence. *Journal of Clinical Child And Adolescent Psychology*, *39*(5), 638–649.

Rapee, R. M., Abbott, M. J., & Lyneham, H. J. (2006). Bibliotherapy for children with anxiety disorders using written materials for parents. *Journal of Consulting and Clinical Psychology*, *74*, 436–444.

Silverman, W. K., & Ginsburg, G. S. (1995). Specific phobias and generalised anxiety disorder. In J. S. March (Ed.), *Anxiety disorders in children and adolescents* (pp. 153–180). New York: The Guilford Press.

Silverman, W. K., Ortiz, C. D., Viswesvaran, C., Burns, B. J., Kolko, D. J., Putnam, F. W., et al. (2008). Evidence-based psychosocial treatments for children and adolescents exposed to traumatic events. *Journal of Clinical Child and Adolescent Psychology*, *37*, 156–183.

Stallard, P., Skryabina, E., Taylor, G., Phillips, R., Daniels, H., Anderson, R., & Simpson, N. (2014). Classroom-based cognitive behaviour therapy: A cluster, randomised-controlled trial to Prevent Anxiety in Children through Education in Schools. *Lancet Psychiatry*, Early Online Publication, 16 July 2014.

Waters, A. M., Groth, T. A., Sanders, M., & O'Brien, R, & Zimmer-Gembeck, M. J. (2015). Developing partnerships in the provision of youth mental health service delivery and clinical education: A school-based cognitive behavioural intervention targeting anxiety symptoms in children. *Behavior Therapy*, 46, 844–855.

Waters, A. M., Ford, L. A., Wharton, T. A., & Cobham, V. E. (2009). Cognitive behavioural therapy for young children with anxiety disorders: Comparison of group-based child + parent versus parent only focused treatment. *Behaviour Research and Therapy*, 47, 654–662.

Waters, A. M., Wharton, T. A., Zimmer-Gembeck, M. J., & Craske, M. G. (2008). Threat-based cognitive biases in anxious children: Comparison with non-anxious children before and after cognitive-behavioural treatment. *Behaviour Research & Therapy*, 46(3), 358–374.

Assessment Module

ASSESSMENT MODULE

Assessment of Anxiety Disorders in Children

Major Activities in this Module

Rapport Building and Socialisation to Treatment

Diagnosis

Diagnostic Interviews

Questionnaire Measures

Program Evaluation

- Evaluation sheets 1 and 2 included at the end of this module

Rapport Building and Socialisation to Treatment

Children are often referred to psychology services by their parents/carers, doctor (general practitioner, paediatrician, psychiatrist), or anxiety symptoms may be identified by a school guidance officer or teacher.

During the assessment phase, it is crucial to gather information and build rapport with each person in the family. For younger children, most of the information gathering can be done with the parents present so as to reduce the pressure on the child. However, it is also important to spend time with the child to allow them to express their thoughts and feelings. Engaging the child in discussion about their favourite activities or situations where they do not feel anxious often assists in the rapport building process. Playing games is a great ice-breaker and we have found children still love playing board games, such as *Guess Who* and *Connect Four*. It is important that children receive praise and encouragement for their efforts in speaking with the practitioner and they may enjoy receiving a sticker or choosing from a 'lucky dip box' to reinforce their efforts and promote a positive experience. Reassuring children about what will happen during the therapy sessions and briefly describing the ACTION plan may further alleviate some of their worries about seeing the practitioner. Often by the second session, children feel more comfortable and they are more willing to discuss their thoughts and feelings. Building this rapport is very important as you will be asking children to face their fears during the Take Action program.

Initially there may be high levels of anxiety experienced by the child and possibly the parents or guardians. Children may want to present positively or give answers they think their parents or the practitioner want to hear, and therefore they may under-report their anxiety symptoms during the assessment process. Children also may not fully understand the nature of anxiety and how it is affecting them. Often parents are happy to bring their children to therapy but it may take longer for them to open up about their own anxiety symptoms and ways in which they may be inadvertently maintaining their child's anxiety (e.g. letting them avoid anxiety-provoking situations). Discuss confidentiality with the family and allow them to discuss their concerns at their pace.

Diagnosis

Differential diagnosis between childhood anxiety disorders can be difficult, due to the high comorbidity rates within the disorders, and also with depressive and externalising disorders. Thus, reliable assessment instruments, which incorporate multiple modalities and reporters, are necessary to enable the multiple facets of childhood anxiety to be addressed. Normal fear and anxiety in children differs from clinically significant anxiety primarily in severity, not in quality. In considering whether anxiety is clinically significant, the guiding principle is determining whether it causes the child marked distress or impairment in important areas of life such as school, social relationships or family functioning. It is important to obtain specific, behavioural descriptions of how the anxiety is interfering in the child's life (i.e., how many areas of the child's life are affected; how many hours of the day does the problem occur), and how excessive or distressing the anxiety is for the child compared with same-aged peers. The duration and pervasiveness of the difficulties and the extent to which they can be controlled are further distinguishing features between clinical and non-clinical anxiety.

Highly detailed and specific information about the specific triggers, frequency, duration, severity and core features of the symptoms is essential when differentiating between anxiety disorder diagnoses. When the presence of concurrent diagnoses has been established, it is important to specify the principal diagnosis (i.e., the disorder that is most problematic in the child's life) and which are the additional diagnoses, in order to tailor the treatment appropriately.

There are several methods of assessment for evaluating anxiety in children, including diagnostic clinical interviews (i.e., structured or unstructured), child-, parent- and teacher-report rating scales and inventories, behavioural observation or avoidance tasks, and physiological recording.

Diagnostic Interviews

The use of structured and semi-structured diagnostic interviews in clinical research and empirically driven clinical practice is highly recommended. Structured or semi-structured diagnostic interviews have several advantages over unstructured interviews, which generally have poor reliability and lack objectivity. Structured interviews increase the reliability of a diagnosis by standardising the content, format and questions to be asked during the interview, and the scoring process for the practitioner. In addition, children appear to respond better to specific questions rather than broad questions.

There are a number of widely used structured diagnostic interview schedules that are appropriate for use in the assessment of childhood anxiety disorders including the:

- Anxiety Disorders Interview Schedule for DSM-IV: Child and Parent Versions (ADIS-C/P; Silverman & Albano, 1996);*
- Child and Adolescent Psychiatric Assessment (CAPA; Angold & Costello, 2000);
- Diagnostic Interview Schedule for Children (DISC; Schwab-Stone et al., 1993);
- Kiddie-Schedule for Affective Disorders and Schizophrenia for School-Age Children (K-SADS; Ambrosini, 2000).

The ADIS-C/P (Silverman & Albano, 1996) is one of the most commonly used diagnostic interview schedules for childhood anxiety. It has a number of beneficial features. Firstly, the importance of obtaining information from children, in addition to significant others, has been emphasised in the literature (Andrews et al., 2003). Children have been shown to provide a unique insight into their own anxiety (Rapee, Wignall, Hudson & Schniering, 2000), and the ADIS-C/P allows for both children and parents to report on anxiety symptoms. Second, the ADIS-C/P relates to DSM-IV criteria (APA, 1994). Both versions have excellent psychometric properties (Silverman, Saavedra & Pina, 2001; Wood, Piacentini, Bergman, McCracken, & Barrios, 2002), and the ADIS-C/P has been shown to possess good sensitivity to treatment effects (Beidel, Turner & Morris, 2000; Hayward et al., 2000; Kendall, 1994; Kendall et al., 1997; Spence, Donovan & Brechman-Toussaint, 2000).

The ADIS-C/P is a clinician-administered semi-structured diagnostic interview, which was developed to establish reliable differential diagnoses among the DSM-IV anxiety disorders and exclusion of alternative diagnoses. Although the ADIS-C/P screens primarily for anxiety disorders, mood disorders and externalising disorders in youth aged 7 to 17 years, it also includes brief screens of other childhood disorders, such as pervasive developmental disorders, somatoform and eating disorders. The anxiety disorders sections address situational and cognitive cues for anxiety, intensity of anxiety, extent of avoidance and the effects on the child.

In addition to providing diagnoses based on child report (via the ADIS-C) and parent report (via the ADIS-P), the interviews provide combined diagnoses (via the ADIS-C and ADIS-P). In administering the interviews, symptoms are judged by the child and parent as being either present (*yes*) or absent (*no*). The total number of *yes* responses is calculated to obtain a total symptom scale score and to determine

*** As of the date of publication the ADIS was still being updated for DSM-V.**

whether the symptoms endorsed meet DSM-IV criteria. If diagnostic criteria are met for a disorder, the child and parent are asked if these symptoms lead to significant clinical interference or impairment. Severity / interference ratings are made by the child and parent using a 9-point scale, ranging from *no interference* (0) to *very severely disabling* (8), provided in the form of a Feelings Thermometer (Silverman & Albano, 1996). To meet DSM-IV criteria for a clinical diagnosis the practitioner assigns a clinician severity rating based on overall symptom severity and impairment. Symptoms are required to have an interference rating of four (*definitely disabling*) or higher. In cases where a child meets criteria for more than one clinical diagnosis, the principal diagnosis is the one that receives the highest clinician severity rating. All other diagnoses meeting diagnostic criteria, but which result in less interference, are referred to as additional.

Questionnaire Measures

Although certain anxiety symptoms, such as avoidance of situations, are readily observable, most symptoms are open only to child introspection and thus self-report. Self-report instruments are designed to be used as an adjunct to a thorough diagnostic interview, and are useful for assessing children's progress during and after the treatment program. The instrument chosen depends on factors such as the age of the child, the type of anxiety reported, and the purpose of the assessment. There are a range of self-report measures designed specifically to assess symptoms of anxiety in children. The following tables list commonly used measures for parents and children. These questionnaires can be used at pre-treatment, mid-treatment and post-treatment, in addition to follow-up sessions.

Parent Questionnaire Measures

Measure	Description	Age range	References
Spence Children's Anxiety Scale (SCAS)	Total score and six subscales related to DSM-IV criteria are provided (generalised anxiety, separation anxiety, social phobia, physical injury fears, panic-agoraphobia, obsessive-compulsive symptoms).	Parent report on children aged 6-18 years (SCAS-P). Parent report on children aged 3-5 years (Preschool Scale; PAS).	Nauta et al. (2004) Spence, Rapee, McDonald & Ingram (2001) For further information see - http://www.scaswebsite.com/
Child Behavior Checklist (CBCL)	Eight problem syndrome scales, in addition to Internalising, Externalising, Total problem behaviour scales are provided.	Parent report for children aged 1.5 – 5 years, and 6 - 18 years.	Achenbach & Edelbrock (1983) Achenbach & Rescorla (2000)
Parenting Scale (PS)	Assesses parenting practices in terms of laxness, verbosity, and over-reactivity subscales.		Arnold, O'Leary, Wolff, & Acker (1993)
Parents Sense of Competency Scale (PSCS)	Parents indicate their agreement with 16 statements regarding parenting satisfaction and self-efficacy.		Johnston & Mash (1989)
Depression, Anxiety and Stress Scale, 42 item version (DASS-42)	Parents report on their own symptoms of Depression, Anxiety and Stress.		Lovibond & Lovibond (1995) For further information see - http://www2.psy.unsw.edu.au /groups/dass/

Child Questionnaire Measures

Measure	Description	Child's Age range	References
Spence Children's Anxiety Scale (SCAS)	Total score and six subscales related to DSM-IV criteria are provided (generalised anxiety, separation anxiety, social phobia, physical injury fears, panic-agoraphobia, obsessive-compulsive symptoms).	6-16 years (SCAS-C)	Spence (1998) For further information see - http://www.scaswebsite.com/
Revised Children's Manifest Anxiety Scale (RCMAS)	Assesses physiological, worry, social anxiety and defensiveness symptoms. Provides inconsistent responding index.	6-19 years	Reynolds and Richmond (1978)
Children's Depression Inventory (CDI)	Assesses depressive symptoms by providing Total score and five subscales (negative mood, interpersonal problems, ineffectiveness, anhedonia, negative self esteem).	7-17 years	Kovacs (1992)

Program Evaluation

It is important that children and parents provide feedback on their treatment satisfaction and learning. Following completion of the Take Action program, children and parents are asked to complete a final evaluation of the program. Using *Evaluation Sheet 1* on page 39, children and parents are asked to rate how much they were satisfied with and had learned from the Take Action program. Two 9-point rating scales are used ranging from 0 (*I didn't like it at all/learn anything*) to 8 (*I liked it/learnt a great deal*).

Using *Evaluation Sheet 2* on page 40, children and parents are asked to rate which treatment strategies (i.e., steps in the ACTION plan) they had found the most useful. Finally, children and parents are given the opportunity to provide any further comments about the program.

References

Achenbach, T. M., & Edelbrock, C. S. (1983). *Manual for the child behavior checklist and profile*. Burlington: University of Vermont, Department of Psychiatry.

Achenbach, T., & Rescorla, L. (2000). *Child behavior checklist*. Burlington, VT: ASEBA.

Ambrosini, P. (2000). Historical development and present status of the Schedule for affective disorders and schizophrenia for school-age children (K-SADS). *Journal of the American Academy of Child and Adolescent Psychiatry, 39*, 49–58.

American Psychiatric Association. (1994). *Diagnostic and statistical manual of mental disorders* (4th ed.). Washington, DC: Author.

Andrews, G., Creamer, M., Crino, R., Hunt, C., Lampe, L., & Page, A. (2003). *The treatment of anxiety disorders: Clinician's guides and patient manuals* (2nd ed). UK: Cambridge University Press.

Angold, A., & Costello, E. J. (2000). The Child and adolescent psychiatric assessment (CAPA). *Journal of the American Academy of Child and Adolescent Psychiatry, 39*, 39–48.

Arnold, D. S., O'Leary, S. G., Wolff, L. S., & Acker, M. M. (1993). The parenting scale: A measure of dysfunctional parenting in discipline situations. *Psychological Assessment*, 5, 137–144.

Beidel, D. C., Turner, S. M., & Morris, T. L. (2000). Behavioral treatment of childhood social phobia. *Journal of Consulting and Clinical Psychology*, 68 (6), 1072–1080.

Hayward, C., Varady, S., Albano, A. M., Thienemann, M., Henderson, L., & Schatzberg, A. F. (2000). Cognitive-behavioural group therapy for social phobia in female adolescents: Results of a pilot study. *Journal of the American Academy of Child and Adolescent Psychiatry, 39*, 721–734.

Johnston, C., & Mash, E. J. (1989). A measure of parenting satisfaction and efficacy. *Journal of Clinical Child Psychology, 18*, 167–175.

Kendall, P. C. (1994). Treating anxiety disorders in children: Results of a randomized clinical trial. *Journal of Consulting and Clinical Psychology, 62*, 100–110.

Kendall, P., Flannery-Schroeder, E., Panichelli-Mindel, S., Southam-Gerow, M., Henin, A., & Warman, M. (1997). Therapy for youth with anxiety disorders: A second randomized clinical trial. *Journal of Consulting and Clinical Psychology, 65* (3), 366–380.

Kovacs, M. (1992). *The Children's depression inventory (CDI) manual.* Toronoto, USA: MultiHealth Systems.

Lovibond, P. F., & Lovibond, S. H. (1995). The structure of negative emotional states: Comparison of the Depression, anxiety and stress scale (DASS) with the Beck depression and anxiety inventories. *Behaviour Research and Therapy, 33* (3), 335–343.

Nauta, M. H., Scholing, A., Rapee, R., Abbott, M., Spence, S. H., & Waters, A. M. (2004). A parent-report measure of children's anxiety: Psychometric properties and comparison with child-report in a clinical and normal sample. *Behaviour Research and Therapy, 42*, 413–439.

Rapee, R. M., Barrett, P. M., Dadds, M. R., & Evans, L. (1994). Reliability of the DSM-III-R childhood anxiety disorders using structured interview: Interrater and parent–child agreement. *Journal of the American Academy of Child and Adolescent Psychiatry, 33*, 984–992.

Rapee, R. M., Wignall, A., Hudson, J. L., & Schniering, C. A. (2000). *Treating anxious children and adolescents: An evidenced based approach.* USA: New Harbinger Publications, Inc.

Reynolds, C. R., & Richmond, B. O. (1978). What I think and feel: A Revised measure of children's manifest anxiety. *Journal of Abnormal Child Psychology*, 6, 271–280.

Schwab-Stone, M., Fisher, P., Piacentini, J., Shaffer, D., Davies, M., & Briggs, M. (1993). The Diagnostic interview schedule for children-revised (DISC-R), II: Test-retest reliability. *Journal of the American Academy of Child and Adolescent Psychiatry, 32*, 651–657.

Silverman, W. K., & Albano, A. M. (1996). *Anxiety disorders interview schedule for DSM-IV: Child and parent versions*. San Antonio, USA: The Psychological Corporation.

Silverman, W. K., Saavedra, L. M., & Pina, A. A. (2001). Test-retest reliability of anxiety symptoms and diagnoses with the Anxiety Disorders Interview Schedule for DSM-IV: Child and parent versions. *Journal of American Academy of Child and Adolescent Psychiatry*, *40*(8), 937–944.

Spence, S. H. (1998). A measure of anxiety symptoms among children. *Behaviour Research and Therapy*, *36*, 545–566.

Spence, S. H., Donovan, C., & Brechman-Toussaint, M. (2000). The treatment of childhood social phobia: The effectiveness of a social skills training-based cognitive-behavioural intervention, with and without parental involvement. *Journal of Child Psychology & Psychiatry & Allied Disciplines*, *41* (6), 713–726.

Spence, S. H., Rapee, R., McDonald, C., & Ingram, M. (2001). The structure of anxiety symptoms among preschoolers. *Behaviour Research and Therapy*, *39*, 1293–1316.

Wood, J., Piacentini, J. C., Bergman, R. L., McCracken, J., & Barrios, V. (2002). Concurrent validity of the anxiety disorders section of the anxiety disorders interview schedule for DSM-IV: Child and parent versions. *Journal of Clinical Child and Adolescent Psychology*, *31*(3), 335–342.

Evaluation Sheet I

Final Evaluation of the Take Action program

Rate on the Feelometer how much you enjoyed the Take Action program (circle your answer below):

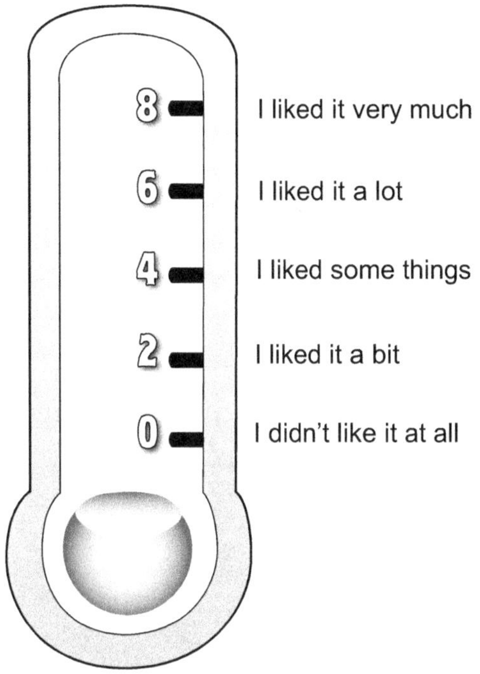

Rate on the Feelometer how much you learnt in the Take Action program:

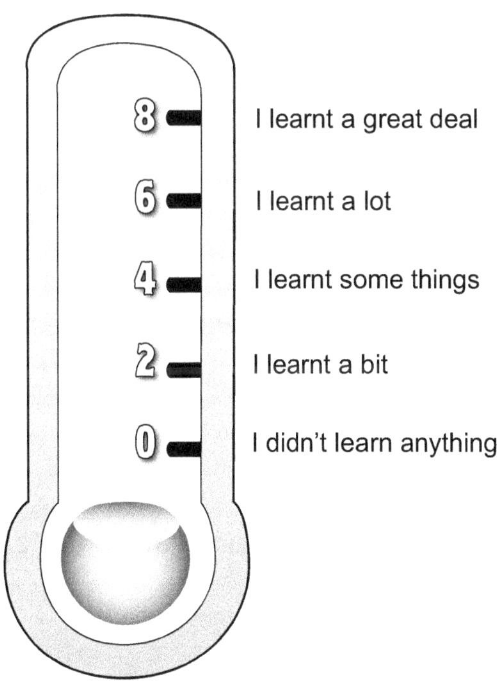

Evaluation Sheet 2

Final Evaluation of the Take Action program

Please rank from 1 (most useful) to 6 (least useful) which steps in the Take Action program you found most useful:

— A **Step One**
I can be **AWARE** of my Anxious Feelings and Body Signals.

— C **Step Two**
I can keep **CALM** by doing On the Spot Deep Breathing and Move My Muscles Relaxation.

— T **Step Three**
I can **THINK** Strong Thoughts.

— I **Step Four**
I can get **INTO** Action by climbing the steps of my Action Ladder and rewarding myself.

— O **Step Five**
I can use my **OPTIONS** including Problem Solving, Strong Team and Focusing on the Positives. I can use my social skills to be more Confident and Assertive, and deal with bullies.

— N **Step Six**
I will **NEVER** stop taking action against anxiety.

Treatment Modules

MODULE 1.1

Introduction to a Take Action Group

Major Activities in this Module

Introduction to the Take Action program

- Handouts *Introduction-1*

Activity Description

The goal of this first session is to help children and parents to settle into the group therapy environment. A brief description of the practitioner's experience in treating childhood anxiety problems can be provided. It is important that children and parents understand the general principles of the Take Action program.

For Children

Facilitate the introductions of each person in the group in a positive way. Colourful name tags depicting the child's favourite sea animal are helpful in the group environment. A fun activity for children initially is The Interview Exercise on handout *Introduction-1*. This activity encourages group members to talk to, and share personal information with other group members. Children are asked to say hello to their partner for the activity, and to take turns in asking the questions listed. Then encourage the children to share their answers in the larger group. A similar exercise can be completed with parents sharing their concerns for their child, and what they would like to achieve during the program.

For Parents and Children

Parent and child group members are also asked to think of rules that will help their group to work well together. The following general group rules may be helpful to start with and then encourage the group members to add other rules.

- Everything talked about in the group is confidential (apart from appropriate limits to confidentiality). Let children know it is okay to talk with parents or friends about their own thoughts and feelings about group activities (e.g., 'we talked about ways to keep calm and relaxed'), but not about what other group members have said.
- There are no right and wrong answers. Let children know it is okay to make mistakes and the activities they will complete are not tests.

- It is okay to have a different idea to someone else. Let children know they do not have to agree with each other all of the time, but it is important to listen to each other and respect other members of the group.
- Share information about yourself only when you feel okay about doing so.

The group rules can be written on a separate page to be displayed in the room, or each group member can write down the rules and staple them inside their handout booklet.

MODULE 1.2

A — Be AWARE

Major Activities in this Module

Introduction to the Take Action program

- Handouts *BeAware-child-1* to *BeAware-child-4*
- Handouts *BeAware-parent-1* to *BeAware-parent-10*

Tools for being AWARE

- Handouts *BeAware-child-5* to *BeAware-child-6*

What to be AWARE of

- Handouts *BeAware-child-7* to *BeAware-child-14*
- Handouts *BeAware-parent-11* to *BeAware-parent-15*

Home tasks and development of reward menu

- Handout *Home Task Reward Chart*
- Handouts *BeAware Home Task One* and *BeAware Home Task Two*

Introduction to the Take Action program

Activity Description

The goal of these exercises is to help children and parents to settle into the therapy environment. A brief description of the practitioner's experience in treating childhood anxiety problems can be provided. It is important that children and parents understand the general principles of the Take Action program.

For Children

What is anxiety?

Use handout *BeAware-child-1* to reassure children that the Take Action program will be fun, and that they will be learning how to take action against their fears and worries. Dulcy and Dion the dolphins are the first sea animals to be introduced, and additional sea animals will be used throughout the program to explain key concepts to children. It is explained to children that anxiety is a common and normal reaction to perceived or real threat in a situation. All children and adults experience anxiety at some stage in their life for different reasons. The different responses to perceived or real threat are discussed, with examples given of a fight response (e.g. children are asked to imagine a caveman fighting off a sabre-tooth tiger), freeze (e.g.

caveman unable to move in the presence of a sabre-tooth tiger), and flight (e.g. cavemen running away from the sabre-tooth tiger). One major feature of children who experience high levels of anxiety is that they tend to avoid anxiety-provoking situations they 'perceive' as being anxiety-provoking when they may not be. In doing so, anxious children have more difficulty learning that things are not as bad as they seem, that the things they are afraid of are often unlikely to happen, and that they can cope.

Use handout *BeAware-child-2A* to brainstorm a list of words related to anxiety. Examples include feeling scared, nervous, afraid, anxious, worried, frightened, fearful, terrified, petrified, and stressed. Younger children may more easily understand the words 'scared' or 'worried'.

ACTION Plan

Using handout *BeAware-child-2B,* explain the six-step ACTION plan that children will learn during the program. The benefits expected to be gained through participation in the program include learning that situations may seem scary but that they are not dangerous, and that children can learn to cope and feel calm in these situations using their ACTION plan.

Read the story on handout *BeAware-child-3.* Ask children the following questions about the story:

- What was Dulcy afraid of? (**Answer:** The swimming teacher's loud voice).
- What was Dion afraid of? (**Answer:** Swimming in the deep end).
- How did Dulcy and Dion take Action against their anxiety? (**Answer:** The dolphins thought Strong thoughts).
- What other things could Dulcy and Dion have done to take Action against their anxiety? (**Answers:** Talk to someone supportive, breathing, relaxation, practice swimming at the pool before their first lesson).

It is important to emphasise the following points:

- That Dulcy and Dion were both going to a swimming lesson but they were scared about different things.
- It is normal to be afraid when things are new and we haven't done them before.
- The dolphins felt better because they thought Strong (helpful) thoughts and this is one way to cope with anxiety.

Use handout *BeAware-child-4* to encourage children to write down situations in which they feel anxious at varying severity levels. Ask children to read through the examples given on the **Worry Wall** to prompt them to think about their own worries. Children are then asked to think of goals they would like to achieve while participating in the program.

For Parents

About the Program

Use handout *BeAware-parent-1* to discuss that the main aim of the Parent Information sessions is to assist parents, to help their child reduce anxiety. Information will be provided on what the child has to do for each step in the ACTION plan, what parents can do to assist their child with each step, and other helpful strategies to reduce anxiety in children. Parents are a very important part of the Take Action program as each parent is very knowledgeable about their own child and how they experience anxiety. Parents are encouraged to be on their child's Strong Team by regularly checking in with their child about what they are learning, and what Home Tasks children are asked to complete.

Use handout *BeAware-parent-2* to explain the structured format of the Take Action program. The content discussed in the Parent Information Sessions parallels what children are learning in their sessions, in addition to what parents can do to help their child with each skill. Use handout *BeAware-parent-3* to discuss the nature of anxiety in children. Emphasise the difference between a child experiencing normal levels of anxiety, and a child who experiences excessive distress or finds it difficult to do things that other children of their age are capable of doing (because of their worries or fears).

Anxiety in children

Use handout *BeAware-parent-4* to explain the different types of anxiety disorders that are targeted in the program: social phobia, generalised anxiety disorder, specific phobias, separation anxiety disorder. Parents should be encouraged to reflect on which type/s of anxiety their child experiences.

Use handout *BeAware-parent-5* to discuss the possible causes and maintaining factors of childhood anxiety. Emphasise that a combination of factors contribute to and currently maintain the child's anxiety. Parents are asked to complete the Causes and Origins activity on handout *BeAware-parent-6*. This is very useful for parents to assist their understanding of the areas that need to be targeted during the program. For example, it would be important for a child who continually avoids anxiety-provoking situations to gradually face their fear through a graduated **Action Ladder**.

Use handout *BeAware-parent-7* to outline how anxiety is expressed in children. The Three Responses of Anxiety in children (i.e., thoughts, somatic symptoms, avoidance) are discussed, and parents are asked whether they have noticed these three responses in their child. It is important that parents are aware of the anxious responses of their child so that they can reinforce the strategies learnt during the program.

Benefits and goals of the program

Use handout *BeAware-parent-8* to outline the benefits expected to be gained through participation in the program. Discuss each step of the ACTION plan, reinforcing the importance of parents encouraging their child's use of each step. Use handout *BeAware-parent-9* to explain how the ACTION plan targets each of the three responses to anxiety. Check parents' understanding of each step in the ACTION plan before moving onto the next activity.

Use handout *BeAware-parent-10* to encourage parents to think of goals they would like their child to achieve during the program, and what goals they would like to achieve personally. Encourage parents to share their goals with their child to ensure the family are already starting to work together as a Strong Team.

Tools for being AWARE

Activity Description

The goal of this exercise is to teach children tools to be more aware of different emotions, including anxiety. Being aware of anxious feelings and body signals, and anxiety-provoking situations is the first step in the ACTION plan.

For Children

Being AWARE of the intensity of anxious feelings

Use handout *BeAware-child-5* to explain the first tool for being aware. The **Feelometer** is a great way to gauge the intensity of an emotion. Although the Feelometer is used primarily in relation to anxiety in this program, it can also be used when discussing the emotions of anger and sadness with children. You should describe the different points on the Feelometer (from cool to boiling hot) and provide examples of anxiety-provoking situations (i.e., anticipatory anxiety, academic or sporting performance, attending school, social appearance, health of child or parent, family problems, events that happen in the world such as natural disasters).

Use handout *BeAware-child-6* to brainstorm anxious situations for each level of the Feelometer. It should be emphasised that people may report different levels on the Feelometer about the same situation.

Being AWARE of biases in attention allocation

As described above in the chapter on the Causes and Maintenance of Anxiety disorders, anxious children show biases in the way they direct attention towards or away from threat stimuli compared to non-anxious children. Some anxious children avoid directing visual attention to threat stimuli, such as an angry face, while others will vigilantly assign visual attention towards the threat for the purposes of threat monitoring. Both processes serve to increase or maintain anxiety. Threat avoidance prevents the opportunity to acquire new information either that the situation is not as threatening as first thought, and/or that the child can cope. Threat vigilance maintains attention on a stimulus that may either be a minor threat or no longer important, both of which interferes with ongoing tasks the child may be engaged in.

Some research evidence suggests that threat avoidance is associated with poorer or slower treatment response to group-based CBT (Waters, Mogg, & Bradley, 2012). Also, recent research suggests that children with phobias are more likely to show threat avoidance compared to children with GAD (Waters, Bradley, & Mogg, 2014). Thus, when conducting exposure-based treatments with children with phobias, it may be important to carefully monitor whether they attempt to avoid looking at the stimulus materials used during exposure, as such avoidance could prevent new learning. Similarly, vigilant monitoring of threat stimuli by young children with GAD may interfere with the child attending to safe/disconfirming cues in the environment and/or remaining focused on other ongoing activities and thus maintain anxiety.

Either way, most anxious children show biased attention allocation in relation to threat stimuli, whether this be towards or away from threat. Although research is underway aimed at altering children's attention processes through attention training (e.g., Eldar et al., 2012), this work is in its infancy and awaits outcomes from carefully controlled trials. Practitioners should encourage anxious children to deploy their attention flexibly to feared stimuli and safe/positive stimuli around them when undertaking exposure therapy as processing both types of stimuli will help establish new learning. We return to this point again in the Keep CALM Module.

What to be AWARE of

Activity Description

Children are encouraged to start being aware of internal (e.g. body signals) and external cues (e.g. facial expressions, reactions of others) when they are in anxiety-provoking situations.

For Children

Anxious Body Signals

Read handout *BeAware-child-7* to explain to children that our bodies are designed to help us if we are in real danger. Our bodies make changes, such as our heart beats faster, to help us feel strong and escape the danger. Explain to children that when we feel anxious about a situation that is scary, but not dangerous, we experience a "false alarm".

Use handout *BeAware-child-8* to discuss how Dulcy identified her anxious body signals. The practitioner should check that the children understand each of the Anxious Body Signals before moving onto the next activity.

Ask children to complete handout *BeAware-child-9* by identifying a situation in which they feel anxious and rate their level on the Feelometer. Encourage children to scan their bodies for clues of changes when they are anxious.

Feelings shown on faces and in body language

Explain the importance of understanding emotions. Explain to children that knowing how they are feeling means they can take ACTION to help themselves go from hot to cool on the Feelometer and stop "false alarms" in the future. It is also important for children to look for external cues in the environment, such as facial expressions and reactions of others. Use Handout *BeAware-child-10* to explore children's understanding of different emotions such as happy, angry, sad, and anxious. Children are asked to name the feelings of the faces depicted in the handout.

Possible feelings shown by the faces include:

- Face 1 — happy, excited, joyful
- Face 2 — angry, aggressive, mean, mischievous
- Face 3 — sad, upset
- Face 4 — frightened, anxious, scared, worried, nervous

Ask children to show each feeling on their face, and then explain how they identified the different feelings. You should explain that it is important to look for clues about whether a situation is scary or dangerous. Children should look at people's eyes and mouth and body language (i.e., how people walk, sit, smile) when looking for clues about a situation. Explain to children that from now on in anxious situations, they can learn to be AWARE of their feelings if they:

1. **Stop.**
2. **Look** for clues in the situation such as people's faces and their body language.
3. **Learn** from their own body signals so they can take Action.

Younger children can be asked to draw each feeling face as an additional activity if you feel this will assist their understanding of the emotions. Use handout *BeAware-child-11(A & B)* to discuss the different sea animals associated with each feeling (i.e. happy, scared, sad, angry, calm). Younger children benefit from making the association between each emotion and the sea animal character. Ask children to identify situations where they have felt like each of the sea animals.

Use handout *BeAware-child-12* and *BeAware-child-13* to further consolidate children's understanding of the concepts covered in the Be Aware step. Ask children to read the two stories and answer the questions.

Read the story on handout *BeAware-child-14* about Dulcy using the Be Aware tools in the future to take Action. Ask children what they have learnt in the Be Aware step and discuss their progress.

For Parents

Parents should be oriented to the concepts covered with children so they know what their children need to be aware of now in anxious situations. Use handout *BeAware-*

parent-11 to explain what anxiety is and how it can be both helpful and harmful, and the concept of anxiety sometimes being a "false alarm" (i.e. a child gets anxious body signals but they are not in a dangerous situation).

Using handout *BeAware-parent-12* explain the Feelometer to parents and encourage them to use the thermometer with their child to assist him/her in identifying varying levels of anxiety in different situations. Encourage parents to complete handout *BeAware-parent-13* to identify situations when children feel calm (Cool) through to extremely anxious (Boiling Hot) on the Feelometer.

Ask parents to complete handout *BeAware-parent-14* by identifying anxious body signals their child commonly experiences.

Use handout *BeAware-parent-15* to discuss different emotions with parents, and how they would know their child was feeling a particular emotion. Parents need to be looking at their child's eyes and mouth and body language (i.e., how they walk, sit, smile). In future anxious situations, parents should encourage their child to:

1. **Stop.**
2. **Look** for clues in the situation based on people's faces and their body language.
3. **Learn** from their Anxious Body Signals so they can take Action.

Parents of younger children should be shown the handout *BeAware-child-11* so they can discuss the feeling sea animal characters with their child. The more the family can associate each sea animal character with the relevant emotion, the easier the child will grasp this important concept.

Parents are shown handout *BeAware-child-12* and *BeAware-child-13* to see their child's answers to these activities. The story by Dulcy on handout *BeAware-child-14* should be discussed with parents to finalise the Be AWARE step.

Home Tasks and Development of Reward Menu

Activity Description

Home Tasks are very important in CBT programs. Children's compliance with Home Tasks is encouraged through the use of a reward system. Home Tasks should be reviewed at the start of each subsequent session to consolidate learning.

For Children

Explain that the purpose of the Home Tasks is to allow children to practice the skills they are learning. Practice of the skills outside of the therapy sessions helps the skills to become automatic and easily used in scary situations. Show the handout *Home Task Reward Chart.* Each session children are given one or more Home Tasks. For each Home Task that is completed and returned to the next session, children will receive a tick from the practitioner on the Reward Chart. The practitioner will sign the Reward Chart each session that a Home Task is completed.

Secondly, children devise a Reward Menu (see handout *BeAware Home Task One*) with their parents. The Reward Menu shows the number of points required for a reward. The rewards can be something to eat (i.e., a favourite chocolate bar or sweet), something to receive (i.e., new pencils) or something to do (i.e., a picnic with the family). Some children might like to save up all their ticks until the last session and then get a big reward. Other children may like to get their rewards throughout the program (for example at week 3, week 6, and week 10).

Use handout *BeAware Home Task Two* to explain the Home Task for this module. Children are asked to use their Be Aware tools to describe different feeling situations.

For Parents

The practitioner explains the Home Tasks and Reward Menu to parents via the handouts *Home Task Reward Chart* and *BeAware Home Task One.* Parents are encouraged to discuss the Home Tasks with their child, and to positively reinforce their efforts in participating during the program. Parents are encouraged to take note of the situations their child lists in the handout *BeAware Home Task Two* so that they can be more AWARE of their child's feelings.

References

Eldar, S., Apter, A., Lotan, D., Perez-Edgar, K., Naim, R., Fox, N. A., Pine, D. S., Bar-Haim, Y. (2012). Attention bias modification treatment for pediatric anxiety disorders: A randomized control trial. *American Journal of Psychiatry*, 169, 213–230.

Waters, A. M. Mogg, K., & Bradley, B. P. (2012). The direction of threat attention bias predicts treatment outcome from cognitive behavioural therapy in anxious children. *Behaviour Research & Therapy*, 50, 428–424.

Waters, A. M., Bradley, B. P., & Mogg, K. (2014). Biased attention to threat in paediatric anxiety disorders (generalized anxiety disorder, social phobia, specific phobia, separation anxiety disorder) as a function of "distress" versus "fear" disorder categorization. *Psychological Medicine*. 44, 607–616.

MODULE 2

C – Keep CALM

Major Activities in this Module

On the Spot Deep Breathing

- Handout *KeepCalm-child-1*
- Handout *KeepCalm-parent-1*

Move My Muscles Relaxation

- Handouts *KeepCalm-child-2* to *KeepCalm-child-4*
- Handout *KeepCalm-parent-2*

Focus on the Positives

Ways to Feel Good

- Handout *KeepCalm-parent-3*

Home Task

- Handouts *KeepCalm-child-5* and *KeepCalm Home Task Three*
- Handout *Home Task Parent*

Bringing the Steps Together

On The Spot Deep Breathing

Activity Description

The goal of this activity is to introduce the second step in the ACTION plan by teaching the **Keep Calm** strategy of **On the Spot Deep Breathing.** The calming strategies taught in the Take Action program are designed to be easy to use, thus increasing the likelihood that the skills will be practiced by children.

For Children

Use handout *KeepCalm-child-1* to explain to children that now they are AWARE of their anxious body signals, they can learn different ways of keeping CALM. Remind children that knowing ways to keep CALM means they are taking action against anxiety. The first way to keep CALM is to practice deep breathing. Breathing can be used 'on the spot', which means it can be practiced in any anxious situation. Children are encouraged to monitor their anxiety levels via the Feelometer, and practice breathing as soon as they feel anxious (Warm on the Feelometer). The quicker children can catch their anxiety and practice a calming strategy, the faster their anxiety will reduce.

Younger children can be encouraged to blow up a coloured balloon as they breathe in, and then imagine the balloon floating into the sky as they breathe out. This can be done for five different coloured balloons as children are encouraged to breathe in and out deeply at least five times. Demonstrate the On the Spot Deep Breathing technique, and then encourage children to practice the skill and assist with its correct implementation. Children are asked to write down times when they could practice the On the Spot Deep Breathing on handout *KeepCalm-child-1*.

For Parents

Demonstrate the On the Spot Deep Breathing using *KeepCalm-parent-1*. Parents are encouraged to practice the skill so that they can assist their child with its correct implementation. It is useful for parents to model the successful use of On the Spot Deep Breathing to their anxious child.

Using the same handout, parents are asked to write down situations in which their child could practice breathing from now on (e.g. separating from a parent to go to school). Parents are encouraged to think about how they would know their child needed to use breathing to keep CALM (e.g. their child starts to breathe very fast), and how they can prompt their child to use this strategy.

Move My Muscles Relaxation

Activity Description

The goal of this activity is to teach the Keep CALM strategy of Move My Muscles Relaxation.

For Children

Use handout *KeepCalm-child-2* to explain to children that our muscles often get stiff and tight when we are anxious (e.g. children often report that they experience neck pain). The second way to keep CALM is to use the **Move My Muscles Relaxation** strategies. Progressive relaxation works really well in getting rid of the tightness in children's muscles. In this relaxation exercise, children are encouraged to tense and then relax each muscle from their face to their feet. Children are encouraged to monitor their anxiety levels via the Feelometer, and practice Relaxation as soon as they feel anxious (Warm on the Feelometer).

Demonstrate the Move My Muscles Relaxation technique and then encourage children to practice the skill and assist with its correct implementation (i.e., counting to 3 while they are tensing each muscle group and then relaxing each muscle group).

Children are asked to write down times when they could practice the Relaxation on handout *KeepCalm-child-2.*

Because relaxation is a sequenced task, children sometimes find a book or card format useful. The handout *KeepCalm-child-3(A & B)* contains six pictures to cut out and make into a set of cards or a small book. This format helps younger children learn the relaxation instructions and they can take the book with them to different anxious situations.

Reinforce the importance of using On the Spot Deep Breathing and Move My Muscles Relaxation whenever children feel anxious. Children are encouraged to focus on the good 'relaxed' feeling when they are practising Keep CALM. Children can practice breathing and muscle relaxation when they are feeling calm, so that their new skills can become an automatic habit. Ask the children if they can remember back to when they first learnt a new skill, such as riding a bike. It may have been hard for children to remember to steer as well as peddle at the same time, but they soon got used to it and it became a habit. Reassure children that the same will happen with their Keep CALM strategies if they practise every day.

Read the story on handout *KeepCalm-child-4* about Dion using the Keep CALM strategies. Ask children what they have learnt in the Keep CALM step and discuss their progress.

For Parents

Demonstrate the Move My Muscles relaxation technique using *KeepCalm-parent-2.* Parents are encouraged to practice the skill so that they can assist their child with its correct implementation. Parents are asked to write down times when their child could practice relaxation. Parents are encouraged to think about how they would know their child needed to use relaxation to keep CALM, and how they can prompt their child to use this strategy.

Focus on the Positives

As reviewed in the Be AWARE Module, anxious children are more likely to direct their attention away from or towards threat stimuli compared with non-anxious children. Therefore, you should encourage anxious children to find and focus their attention on safe cues and/or positive stimuli in the environment as a means of keeping CALM. This is important for gaining evidence that most situations are safe, and that harm to the child is unlikely. If children fail to process the safe cues, new learning about the situation and their coping ability can be impaired.

For example, a child who is fearful of dogs, may initially focus attention on a dog opening his mouth and bearing his teeth, and then avoid looking at the dog. However, the child should be encouraged to shift attention back to the dog and towards signals of safety and positivity such as the dog wagging his tail, signalling he wants to play. For children with storm and weather worries, for example, they may vigilantly scan the sky for storm clouds in the playground at lunchtime. However, they should be encouraged to note the movements of the clouds, observing that they might be moving away and to stay focused on positive events such as playing with their friends. Thus, encouraging flexible deployment of attention between fear stimuli and safe/positive stimuli is helpful during exposure therapy and is discussed again in the Get INTO Action Module.

Ways to Feel Good

Activity Description

It is important that children practice On the Spot Deep Breathing and Move My Muscles Relaxation to keep CALM. However, it is also helpful if anxious children spend more time 'feeling good' and being engaged in positive activities that they enjoy. This activity encourages parents to think about 'feel good' and calming activities that can become part of their child's everyday life.

For Parents

Explain that learning to 'feel good' helps children to keep CALM and to focus less on the negative aspects of the situation (i.e., what they fear) and more on the safe/positive aspects. Children also learn that anxiety is not the only feeling they can experience, and that positive feelings, such as happiness, are enjoyable. Using handout *KeepCalm-parent-3*, ask the parents to read through the list of 'feel good' activities and indicate which of these activities their child would enjoy. Encourage parents to combine these activities into their child's everyday life.

Home Task

Activity Description

This Home Task requires children to practice their Keep CALM strategies of On the Sport Deep Breathing and Move My Muscle Relaxation at least once every day. It is important for children to continue to practise the Keep CALM strategies from this module onwards.

For Children

As part of the Home Task, children are asked to think about when they will practice the Keep CALM strategies. Use handout *KeepCalm-child-5* to explain to children that they need to circle what time of the day they will practice their strategies. Children are also asked to think of anything that may stop them from practising the deep breathing and muscle relaxation, and ways to prevent that happening.

Using handout *KeepCalm Home Task Three*, explain to the children that this Home Task encourages them to practice their On the Spot Deep Breathing and Move My

Muscles Relaxation at least once every day. You should explain the monitoring chart to the children using the following points:

- For each day of the week, children tick the box if they completed their breathing and relaxation practice.
- Children rate their Feelometer level before and after practising breathing and relaxation.

For Parents

Explain the Home Tasks via handouts *KeepCalm-child-5* and *KeepCalm Home Task Three.* Parents are encouraged to discuss the Home Tasks with their child, and positively reinforce their efforts at practising the Keep CALM strategies.

Introduce parents to the **Parent Monitoring Diary** using the handout *Home Task Parent.* It is useful for parents to continue monitoring their child's anxiety levels throughout the entire Take ACTION program via this diary. Explain the Monitoring Diary covering the important points below:

- Each time parents notice their child is anxious, write down the date, time, and describe the anxious situation.
- Parents rate their child's anxiety level on the Feelometer. Parents could also ask their child to rate their own anxiety level.
- Parents note how they knew that their child was anxious (i.e., noticed their child's anxious body signals of sweating and shaking).
- Parents record what their child said and did in the situation (i.e., did they avoid?).
- Parents report what they did in the situation (e.g. 'I prompted my child to practice On the Spot Deep Breathing').

Practitioners may wish to photocopy the monitoring diary for repeated use with parents. At the beginning of each session, the practitioner should discuss the diary to review the progress of the child and parent during the Take ACTION Program.

Bringing the Steps Together

The major sequence of steps to work through with children up to this point in the Take Action program is as follows:

a. Be AWARE of anxiety triggers and anxious body signals
b. Keep CALM by using On the Spot Deep Breathing and Move My Muscles Relaxation

MODULE 3

T — THINK Strong Thoughts

Major Activities in this Module

Explaining the Relationship Between Thoughts–Feelings–Actions

- Handouts *Thoughts-child-1* to *Thoughts-child-3*

Strategies for Helping Children Catch Their Thoughts

- Handouts *Thoughts-child-4* to *Thoughts-child-7 and Thoughts Home Task Four*

Strategies for Helping Children to Find Strong Thoughts

- Handouts *Thoughts-child-8* to *Thoughts-child-12*
- Handout *Thoughts-parent-1*

Strategies for Helping Children to Keep 'Strong' Thoughts

- Handouts *Thoughts-child-13* to *Thoughts-child-14*
- Handout *Thoughts-parent-2 (A, B, C)*
- Handout *Thoughts Home Task Five*

Bringing the Steps Together

Explaining the Relationship Between thoughts–feelings–actions

Activity Description

The goal of this exercise is to help children understand that the way they feel and act are influenced by the way they THINK. Children learn that thoughts, feelings, and actions are different, and that scared thoughts will make them feel scared, and avoid things (actions). In contrast, strong thoughts will help them feel CALM (feeling) and to take ACTION. **Thinking Strong Thoughts** is the third step in the ACTION plan.

For Children

Note: When working with children aged 4 to 7 years, practitioners should consider the appropriateness of the content in the Think Strong Thoughts module, and only use handouts and techniques that are appropriate for the child's age and understanding.

Use handout *Thoughts-child-1* to show children that the way they THINK (which is represented by the thought bubble) can change how they feel (which is represented by the heart) and what they do (which is represented by the star) because their thoughts always come first.

Use handout *Thoughts-child-2* to illustrate how children can think about the same situation differently. Ask children to read aloud each animal's thoughts and to write down the feeling each animal would have because they thought that way. Integrating skills from prior modules, encourage the child to identify clues on each animal's face or from their body language that suggests what type of feeling they might be experiencing. Prompt children to tell you these clues out loud.

Answers for this activity are:

- Dianne the Duck felt anxious, worried, scared, frightened.
- Freddie the Fish felt angry, mad, mean.
- Sammy the Starfish felt happy, relieved.

Use handout *Thoughts-child-3* to encourage children to identify times when they felt scared, angry, and happy. Integrating skills from prior modules, encourage children to rate the intensity of their feeling using the Feelometer (feelings), what they thought in the situation, and what they did in that situation (action).

Psychoeducation about thoughts

Highlight to children that thoughts can take the form of either words or pictures in their mind. Children might see a scary image or hear themselves verbalising scary things, and both are reflective of scared thoughts. Explain how children can THINK a number of different ways about a situation — scared, calm, angry — and that they can *choose* which way they want to THINK, even if it feels like the scary thought which comes to mind first, is really strong and powerful. It is important for children to learn that 'thoughts are just thoughts' and they will pass, or they can Take Action to help get rid of scary thoughts. Help children to learn that once they recognise scary thoughts, they have options. They can ignore the scary thought, because it is just a thought and may not be reality, or they can 'test out' their thoughts and look for clues that tell them that scary thoughts are unlikely. It is helpful to explain to children that their brains are very clever and can think up a wide range of things including things that can seem scary. The important message is for children to learn not to be afraid of their thoughts.

Explain to children how they are going to learn skills to catch scared thoughts, find Strong thoughts, and keep Strong thoughts. Add that just like riding a bike, the more children practice, the better they will become at catching scared thoughts, finding strong ones and keeping them. Therefore, encourage children to pay attention to their thinking in general — whether scary, happy or calm.

For Parents

Based on learning principles, parents should be oriented to the concepts covered with children so they can reinforce them. At the end of the session with children, parents should be shown the handouts of *Thoughts-child-1* to *Thoughts-child-3* so they can see their child's progress and the types of thoughts they experienced.

Parents should encourage their children to talk about their thoughts and to avoid catastrophising or conversely minimising children's scary thoughts, even if they can seem quite disturbing. Parents should be instructed to acknowledge, empathise with, and normalise children's thoughts. For example: 'I can see that thought makes you feel scared. Everyone has scary thoughts, including me, but thoughts are just thoughts and will not harm you. Let's watch and see'.

Parents own scary thoughts

Given the increased likelihood of anxious children having an anxious parent, remind parents of the importance of withholding the verbalisation of their own scary thoughts in front of children. Parents may sometimes have concerns about this, believing that pointing out potential dangers helps keep their children safe from harm. The first major point to be emphasised is that most situations in which children feel anxious are objectively safe situations that typically many other children of a similar age are able to manage with. Therefore there is often no or very little risk to be pointed out. The second is that inflating threat salience of situations may be *more* likely to make the situation seem dangerous to anxious children. This is because they are more likely to avoid or escape these situations, which in turn makes the situation seem scary to children and one they cannot cope with. For example, a parent who has a phobia of water, and thus, swimming, the beach and pools, may be inclined to verbalise threat about these situations (e.g. 'you could drown') because they are afraid themselves. Learning to swim is a safe activity for children and can prevent children from drowning. Therefore, parents should be encouraged to focus attention on positive and safe clues in situations involving their child (e.g., children smiling and enjoying swimming). This includes looking for objective information about the probability of risk and danger actually occurring (e.g., children are safe; there are teachers nearby), and to verbalise those stimuli to their children (e.g., 'look at the faces of all the kids — they are smiling and enjoying it and everyone is safe'), thereby drawing their child's attention to these positive and safe stimuli as well.

Strategies for Helping Children Catch Their Thoughts

Activity Description

The aim of this activity is to help children learn ways to identify anxious thoughts. It can be difficult for children to know what they are thinking so it is important to help them utilise strategies for doing this. Children will learn to catch anxious thoughts by being aware of when they feel anxious; using a DVD player analogy to 'rewind' their minds back to find thoughts that made them feel anxious; and by keeping a thoughts diary of a range of different emotional situations, including happy, anxious and calm.

For Children

Catching thoughts by being AWARE

Using handout *Thoughts-child-4*, explain how people can think about the same situation differently and that by being AWARE of their own anxious body signals, children can catch scared thoughts. Use handout *Thoughts-child-5A* to explain the impact of Scared Thoughts. Then using handout *Thoughts-child-5B*, ask children to write down a recent time they felt anxious (e.g., going upstairs on my own). Prompt them to record what anxious body signals they remember having (e.g., heart was racing). Then ask them what made them feel scared in that situation (e.g., there might be a stranger up there). If the child identifies the source of threat only, additionally ask 'what did you think was going to happen in that situation?' (e.g., 'they would attack me'). Record the child's thoughts on the handout and highlight that by being aware of anxious body signals, this tells children to ask themselves 'what am I scared of', which in turn, enables them to catch anxious thoughts. Describe scared thoughts to children via the handout. Explain that once children can catch scared thoughts, they can take action to THINK Strong thoughts.

The next activity to help children catch thoughts involves showing children the picture of the growling dog in handout *Thoughts-child-6*. Explain to the child that the activity is to give them more practice at being aware of their body signals and their thoughts. Show them the picture and on handout *Thoughts-child-6*, ask the child to record on the handout any anxious body signals they experience, and to tell you what thoughts come to mind, and what do they think would happen if they saw a growling dog like the one in the picture. Children's answers to these questions are their thoughts and beliefs triggered by the picture.

Catching thoughts by rewinding your mind!

In this activity, children learn that our brains are like DVD players. They record a lot of information which we can rewind to recall what we were thinking about. This can be helpful if children become anxious and did not identify this at the time. They are encouraged to 'play back' an event, describing it to you (or a parent), to identify the way they thought about the situation at the time. Use handout *Thoughts-child-7* to explain this to children.

Catching thoughts: Keeping a Thoughts Diary

Explain to children that we get better at catching our thoughts by practising (even with all sorts of different thoughts, such as those we have at happy and calm times). Ask children to record information in the handout *Thoughts Home Task Four* about two scary times they have experienced. Younger children can be encouraged to draw scary situations, or their parents can write down their answers for them.

For Parents

Explain to parents the activities that were covered with children via handouts *Thoughts-child-4* to *Thoughts-child-7*. The handout *Thoughts Home Task Four* should be explained to parents to ensure children complete this between sessions. Parents should be encouraged to monitor signs of anxious body signals in children, particularly in situations known to make their child anxious, and to use the following prompts to help children identify anxious thinking:

- What are you afraid is going to happen?
- What made you feel scared in that situation?
- If your anxious body signals could talk, what would they say about this situation?

Parents should also review situations in which their child became anxious by using the DVD player analogy to encourage children to review the situation and thoughts they experienced. Once again, parents should be encouraged to be non-judgemental about their child's thoughts and instead, acknowledge them, and their child's efforts at being aware of their feelings and thoughts, and move onto steps to promote strong thoughts described below. Parents should additionally monitor their own body signals and anxious thinking and avoid verbalising those thoughts to their children.

Strategies for Helping Children Find Strong Thoughts

Activity Description

Once children learn how to catch Scared thoughts, it can be helpful to teach them how to find Strong thoughts based on whether their anxious thinking tends to be characterised by themes of overestimation of risk and danger in a situation, underestimation of one's ability to cope, and concerns about their own thinking (i.e., worrying about worrying).

Overestimation of risk/danger refers to perceiving a situation or event as more dangerous and threatening than it really is. In this case, the error in thinking tends to be about factors external to the child, and often occurs in response to mild threats or in ambiguous situations. For example, a child who sees dark clouds in the sky may think 'there is going to be a bad storm' (overestimating risk of a bad storm when the clouds may just be rain clouds). Another example is the child who sees someone frown and thinks 'that person is angry' or even 'that person is angry at me' (overestimating the person is angry when they could be thinking about something else). Therefore, overestimation of risk/danger refers to an inflated probability of a dangerous event happening, when in reality, the probability is lower than expected.

Underestimation of coping refers to the perception the child will not be able to cope effectively or tolerate distress in a situation. This typically relates to thoughts about the child themselves (e.g., 'I am not good enough; I will say something silly'), and often relates to more challenging situations that may require active coping but for which the child underestimates their ability. For example, some anxious children may underestimate their ability in perceived performance situations, such as giving a talk in class, speaking in front of others, trying a new activity, or coping (i.e., not becoming distressed and upset) or when faced with their feared objects. As long as anxious children avoid feared situations, they will be reinforcing underestimations of coping by not gaining evidence that they can cope and/or tolerate distress.

Concern about their own thinking refers to thoughts, whereby some children might think there is something wrong with them if they have bad or scary thoughts; or that if they think about something scary, then it must be true; or that if they have a scary thought, they should try to stop themselves thinking that way. For these thinking errors, it is important to work on de-emphasising the threat value children place on their thinking.

For Children

When looking at the child's thought diary as well as the thoughts they describe during the session, evaluate whether they reflect an overestimation of risk/danger, underestimations of coping, or worry about their own thinking. This is useful when deciding what activities are used to encourage the child to find Strong Thoughts (*Thoughts-child-8*). For example, for overestimations of risk/danger, finding Strong Thoughts might relate to finding thoughts that are more likely explanations for the situation. For underestimations of coping, the focus might be on finding Strong Thoughts that emphasise coping, being strong and persisting.

Finding strong thoughts: Targeting Overestimations of risk/danger

As a rule of thumb, if the child describes thoughts reflective of overestimation of risk/danger, focus on working with the child to establish the realistic probability of the feared event happening. In almost all cases, the probability is likely to be small because anxiety is often driven by threat-based thinking, rather than realistic appraisal of the situation. Moreover, if the probability of the negative event is high, then the focus should be on assisting the child to cope in that situation.

For thoughts reflecting on overestimation of risk/danger, use handout *Thoughts-child-9* to provide an example and to encourage the child to evaluate the probability of a scary event occurring. The handout contains a pie graph, in which the child identifies one piece of the pie as being the outcome they expect to happen. Ask the child to generate other possibilities that could happen. Then in the table, assist the child to identify clues each outcome could be true and clues they could be false. Then, tick which outcome is the most likely.

Next using handout *Thoughts-child-10*, ask the child to complete the pie chart about one of their own scary thoughts. Assist them to identify other options, the clues for and against each option, and then decide which option is more likely. Thus, when children catch Scared Thoughts, remind them to say to themselves "How likely is that?" It will prompt them to find Strong thoughts.

Note that if the event has happened before and the child experienced the feared outcome, it is important to focus the child on their experience of the feared outcome. That is, highlighting that the worst has happened and that they managed through it, even if it was unpleasant. You can also point out that in a sense, 'the worst is over' because the most feared outcome has happened, meaning there is less to be afraid of in terms of the small probability that the event will occur again. Additionally, it would be helpful to have the child develop a coping plan for what they would do if the event did happen again, as outlined below.

Finding strong thoughts: Targeting underestimations of coping

Underestimation of coping thoughts typically occurs in situations where the child might be expected to experience some distress and anxiety. For example, a child who is fearful of the dentist will likely be distressed by having a dental visit and will underestimate their ability to manage in that situation (e.g., 'I'll get so scared I'll faint'). In these situations, it is important to develop a coping ACTION Plan with the child, such as the one in handout *Thoughts-child-11*. This can include Keep CALM techniques; focusing on nice, safe cues; using On The Spot Deep Breathing or Move My Muscles techniques, such as hand squeezing or foot rolls. Children should also generate Strong Thoughts focused on the fact that the situation will not last for long and that they can cope.

It is also important to keep in mind that situations in which children underestimate their coping are often situations in which they might also overestimate risk/danger. Therefore, it may be important to both address risk overestimations (i.e., in most cases, dental visits involve routine checkups and are time-limited) and work on a child developing a coping plan in the situation.

Finding strong thoughts: Think of all the options

It can sometimes be difficult for anxious children to identify thoughts other than a scary one, because their scared thought feels very powerful and strong. Therefore, once anxious children have a scared thought, they may not search for other thoughts that could also explain a situation. Use handout *Thoughts-child-12*, to help children generate lots of different ways of thinking about a situation, to classify them into Scared or Strong thoughts, and to consider the consequences if they followed each type of thought. Encourage children to review which thoughts and consequences are the best. The major goal in this activity is to encourage children to look for several different ways of appraising a situation, and to decide which one to follow by looking at what the consequences are.

Finding strong thoughts: Targeting concern about thinking

In relation to children being concerned about their own thoughts it is helpful to work through the following activities.

(a) For children who think it is scary to think about bad thoughts, simple psychoeducation about the human brain can be helpful. Explain that the human brain is like a computer and can do very complicated and clever things. This includes making thoughts that are both very nice, very calm, very angry, very scary and very exciting. However, often we don't pay attention to the nice or calm thoughts, just the scary ones. Therefore, it is not that the child has more bad than good thoughts, they just pay more attention to them. It also is helpful to point out that everyone has all sorts of different thoughts and that some people think their bad thoughts are scary, while others do not feel alarmed by them.

(b) With that in mind, encourage children to learn that sometimes it is okay to ignore their thoughts. It is often helpful to point out that thinking something will not make it come true. In other words, our thoughts are not linked to reality. The Cheeseburger Thoughts activity is helpful with this. Ask the child to tell you what their favourite food is, such as a Cheeseburger, as one child told us when doing this activity. Then ask them to close their eyes and think about that image in great depth: prompt them to tell you what it smells like, what it tastes like, feels like and looks like. Do this for several minutes and in great detail. Ask them to try really hard to focus on their favourite food and to see if that makes their favourite food appear. It is the same with scary thoughts: bad things will not happen just because a child thinks about them. Thus, a major goal of this section is to encourage children to de-emphasise the significance of threat-based thinking and to identify Strong Thoughts based on active, coping self-statements that keep their attention focused on nice things in their environment and on their activities at hand.

For Parents

Explain to parents the content of what has been covered in the session with their child. Outline the three common thinking styles of overestimation of risk/danger, underestimation of coping and concern about their thinking. Use handout *Thoughts-parent-1* to encourage parents to recall times they can remember their child thinking each of these ways. It is helpful to go through handouts *Thoughts-child-8* through *Thoughts-child-12* so parents are aware of the strategies children have learnt for challenging overestimations of risk/danger, developing coping plans, and dealing with concern about their thoughts. Encourage parents to work on helping their child to re-evaluate the probability of a dangerous outcome eventuating in situations in which they overestimate risk, and encourage them to develop task-focused action plans for managing through situations they feel anxious about.

It can be helpful to ask parents to take note of their own thinking styles, to employ similar strategies for correcting this thinking and to avoid expressing anxious thoughts to their child. Instead, parents should be encouraged to share a strong thought, which is outlined in the next activity.

Strategies for Helping Children to Keep Strong Thoughts

Activity Description

The aim of this activity is to ensure children have a concrete way of remembering what their Strong thoughts are following the various activities above.

For Children

Strength Sayings

Identifying problematic thinking themes such as overestimation of risk/danger and underestimation of coping, provide insights into the types of Strong thoughts children can be encouraged to focus on. For example, if a child is worried about running late for school (overestimation of risk), a Strong thought would be 'I rarely run late, and even when I have, everything has been fine' (realigning the probability of risk based on prior experience). For children whose thinking reflects on underestimations of coping, which typically occurs in situations children find challenging, Strong thoughts should focus on anxiety being time-limited and manageable. For example, for children who find talking in front of the class to be difficult, a Strong thought could be 'this won't take very long and I can handle that'. For children who worry about their thinking, Strong thoughts can be 'it's just a thought, not reality', 'throw it away', 'in one ear and out the other'. Moreover, catchy 'Strength Sayings' can be used that help remind children to keep focused on Strong Thoughts and helpful action they can take. Use handout *Thoughts-child-13* to review a range of catchy Strength Sayings that target different types of thinking themes. Strength Sayings 1-2 target overestimations of risk/danger, 3-5 target underestimations of coping, 6-9 target concerns about thinking, 10-11 target worrying, and 12-13 target avoidance. Encourage children to circle and practice Strength Sayings that relate to the kinds of thinking themes that underlie their Scared Thoughts.

Strength Cards

Once children have identified relevant Strong thoughts, it is helpful for children to translate these thoughts onto Strength Cards. This can be decorated with stickers in session and helps to reinforce the Strong thoughts children have identified (see handout *Thoughts-child-14*). Children should be encouraged to carry their Strength Cards with them in anxiety-provoking situations, and to keep them in places where they will see their Strength Card often, such as beside their bed, or as a bookmark for reading. Use the handout *Thoughts Home Task Five*, to encourage children to develop a Strength Card at home, which relates to a situation they find anxiety-provoking. Children should bring this Strength Card to their next session. Strength cards work very well with younger children who can draw pictures of them thinking and acting in a strong way.

For Parents

Explain to parents the activities that were covered with children via handouts *Thoughts-Child-13* to *Thoughts-Child-14*. Encourage parents to help their child develop a coping plan in situations they consider to be anxiety–provoking. This should include developing a Strength Card, and parents could be encouraged to help their child identify their Strong thought and create their Strength Card.

Use handout *Thoughts-parent-2 (A, B, C)* to discuss effective parenting strategies for increasing strong behaviour, and decreasing anxious behaviour. Discuss which strategies parents are already using with their child, and reinforce the strategies the parent needs to use from now on.

Bringing the Steps Together

The major sequence of steps to work through with children up to this point in the program is as follows:

a. Be AWARE of anxiety triggers and anxious body signals
b. Keep CALM by using On the Spot Deep Breathing and Move My Muscles Relaxation
c. Catch scared thoughts
d. Look for thinking themes: overestimation of risk/danger, underestimation of coping, concern about thinking
e. Find Strong thoughts that target these thinking themes
f. Keep Strong thoughts through Strength Sayings and Strength Cards

Module 4

I – Get INTO Action

Major Activities in this Module

Explaining the Importance of Getting INTO Action

- Handouts *IntoAction-child-1* to *IntoAction-child-2*
- Handouts *IntoAction-parent-1* to *IntoAction-parent-3*

Developing an ACTION Ladder and Rewards

- Handouts *IntoAction-child-3* to *IntoAction-child-5*

Example ACTION Ladder

What to do When Completing a Step on the Action Ladder In-session

Reviewing ACTION Ladders

- Handouts *IntoAction Home Task Six* and *IntoAction Home Task Seven*

Bringing the Steps Together

Explaining the Importance of Getting INTO Action

Activity Description

The goal of this exercise is to help children understand that anxiety keeps going because children avoid situations that make them feel scared. Therefore, if children face the situations or stimuli they are afraid of, they will find out that these situations are not as bad as they thought (see *overestimations of risk* in the prior module), and that they can cope (see *underestimations of coping* in the prior module). The best way for children to face their fears is to set a goal and break it down into small steps. We call this **Getting INTO Action.** This is the fourth step in the ACTION Plan.

For Children

Use handout *IntoAction-child-1* to explain to children what it means to get INTO Action. This is a story about Dulcy (the dolphin) and it demonstrates how she sets a goal of swimming by herself, and achieves this goal by breaking it down into small steps. Prior to this session, retrieve the child's main Take Action goals from module 1 (e.g., going to camp; walking to class without mum; going to bed by myself). Select one of these goals and using handout *IntoAction-child-2*, work together to identify small steps the child can achieve in a gradual way until they reach the goal.

For Parents

Parents can sometimes feel concerned about their child having to face situations that make them anxious. It is therefore helpful to provide a good rationale about the role of exposure therapy prior to beginning this work. Use handout *IntoAction-parent-1* with parents to help explain why it is important for children to practice approaching scary situations. Also review handout *IntoAction-parent-2(A & B)* with parents to discuss important tips for how to set up an Action ladder successfully. Finally, work through handout *IntoAction-parent-3*, which sets out some common obstacles in creating and successfully carrying out Action Ladders.

Developing an ACTION Ladder and Reward Card

Activity Description

The major goal of this activity is to develop an exposure hierarchy — referred to as an ACTION Ladder — which includes steps the child can progressively achieve. ACTION Ladders need to be practical and easy to implement both in session and between sessions.

For Children

Select one of the child's Take Action goals and using handout *IntoAction-child-3* record this goal at the top of the ladder. Then use handout *IntoAction-child-4* to identify small steps the child can achieve in a gradual way until they reach the goal. It is helpful to encourage a brainstorming approach whereby the child and the practitioner identify different steps (about 6–8 steps maximum) that could fit into the ladder. Next, have the child use the Feelometer to rank how anxiety provoking each step would be for them. Then using these rankings as a guide, transfer the step with the lowest fear rating to the bottom step of the ladder on handout *IntoAction-child-3*. Then, place progressively harder (more anxiety-provoking) steps one above the other. It is helpful to explain to the child that they will work through the steps gradually and only move onto the next step when they feel Calm (or Cool on the Feelometer) practising the previous step.

Explain that they will practice some of their steps in-session with you and also at home with their parents. It is also helpful to add that getting INTO Action and facing their fears is just like riding a bike. The more often you do it, the easier it gets, so lots of practice is really helpful.

Children may show distress about completing the ACTION Ladder and facing situations they are afraid of. It is important to reassure the child they can work through the steps slowly, and that they are not facing their feared situation straight away. It is helpful to remind children they will be taking it one step at a time, while using the new skills they have learnt. In these cases, children are focussing on the final target goal rather than on the first step in the ACTION Ladder. It may be beneficial to ask the child how anxious they feel using the Feelometer about facing their feared situation (i.e., the target goal). Then ask them how anxious they feel about the first step on the ladder. This is likely to be much less (or you can point to their rating during the brainstorming exercise), to highlight that they only need to focus on one step at a time. It can be helpful to remind the child of the Strength Saying 'keep your mind where your body is', which means to focus on the tasks at hand rather than in the future. This is one of the Strength Sayings covered in the THINK Strong Thoughts Module.

For Children and Parents Together

Once an ACTION Ladder has been developed with the child, it is helpful to review the ladder on handout *IntoAction-child-3* with parents and children together. The main goal is to identify the practicalities involved in organising each step, such as the time and day the next step can be practiced, and any materials that might be required. For example, for the first step of looking at pictures of dogs for a child with a specific phobia of dogs, this might be obtaining relevant picture stimuli. This activity should also identify any obstacles that might interfere with completing each step and potential solutions.

Organise the ACTION Ladder so that steps can be conducted in-session and between-session. It can be helpful if the first few steps on the ladder can be conducted in-session where you can have greater control over the session and parents have an opportunity to observe the process.

It is also important that children's progress on the ACTION Ladder is acknowledged. This can be with praise, physical affection from parents, such as a hug or a 'high-5', or through various small rewards. Handout *IntoAction-child-5* assists children to think of potential rewards they can receive at each step of their ACTION Ladder. The potential rewards can then be discussed with parents. Using handout *IntoAction-child-3*, explain to children and parents how the rewards for achieving each step should be recorded alongside the goal in each step.

Children should continue exposure therapy (i.e., ACTION Ladders), both in-session and between-session, throughout the remainder of treatment. This could mean that children complete more than one ACTION Ladder during treatment (Waters, Potter, Jamesion, Bradley, & Mogg, 2015).

Example ACTION Ladder

Activity Description

The main purpose of this section is to provide an example ACTION Ladder.

Specific Phobia: Dogs

Step 1: Child and Practitioner sit on the other side of the room from the dog (while it is on the lead).

Step 2: Child describes the dog and its behaviour, noting how the dog moves (e.g., wagging tail, panting, lying down, sniffing etc). Practitioner provides psycho-education about dog behaviour, highlighting cues from the dog that indicate he/she is calm/restful, playful, or threatened. Also provide information about how to approach a dog, and conditions when a dog should be left alone (e.g., eating, sleeping).

Step 3: Move closer to the dog (e.g., halfway across the room). Child continues describing the dog's behaviour.

Step 4: Practitioner approaches dog and greets it, then begins patting the dog. Child continues describing dog's behaviour.

Step 5: Child stands beside Practitioner and observes patting. Child continues describing dog's behaviour.

Step 6: Child stands beside Practitioner while Practitioner pats the dog. Child continues describing dog's behaviour.

Step 7: Child places hand on Practitioner's forearm or wrist while Practitioner pats the dog. Child continues describing dog's behaviour.

Step 8: Child places hand under Practitioner's hand while patting the dog together. Child continues describing dog's behaviour.

Step 9: Practitioner removes their hand while remaining beside the child as they pat the dog alone. Child continues describing dog's behaviour.

Step 10: Let dog off the lead. Child continues describing dog's behaviour.

Step 11: Both dog and child move around the room freely until child feels comfortable. Child continues describing dog's behaviour.

Step 12: Move through Steps 3–9 with dog off the lead.

Other exposure options after initial success include:

- Expose child to variety of dogs in terms of size, colour, and temperament.
- Conduct exposure outdoor and in a variety of settings (e.g., park; friend's house).
- Ensure exposure occurs regularly between sessions.
- Where possible, clear the room of chairs and tables or other furniture to avoid the child retreating to these stimuli which herald safety/avoidance/escape.
- It may be helpful to place markers on the floor (i.e., 'stepping stones') between the child and the dog to provide clear markers of where the child can step forward to next.

What to do When Completing a Step on the ACTION Ladder In-session

- Ensure you have the stimulus materials required for completing the exposure task (e.g., pictures or actual stimuli; e.g., dog; darkened room; thunderstorm sounds and DVDs) and a suitable room or other location for the session (e.g., stair-well; elevator).
- Revise the ACTION Ladder with the child and highlight the step they will be working on in that session.
- Remind the child they can take their time and to use the strategies they have been learning as part of their ACTION plan as they gradually confront the feared object or situation. This might include reminding them to use **On the Spot Deep Breathing** or **Move my Muscles Relaxation**; to verbalise their **Strength Sayings**; and to use their **Strength Cards.**
- Take Feelometer ratings before each exposure begins.
- Set the stimulus in front of the child.
- Begin to engage in conversation about the stimulus and the child's reactions. Remind the child that at this stage you just want them to watch the stimulus and to tell you what is going on. Ask the child to tell you everything about the stimulus and how they are feeling. Ask them to describe what they see, what anxious body signals and scared thoughts they might be experiencing.
- Use psycho-education to target overestimations of risk (e.g., 'see how after your eyes get accustomed to the dark, you can see a little bit more but you've got to wait a few minutes for your eyes to adjust to the dark for that to happen') and underestimations of coping (e.g., 'look, you are on the ladder and you are very sturdy; you are patting the dog and look confident').
- Target attention biases by directing the child to look at the feared stimulus directly, and by pointing out the safe and positive clues for the child to focus on. These may relate either to the stimuli or to the child's coping (e.g., 'Look at the dentist's face, he is smiling' — risk overestimation; 'you are feeling uncomfortable but nothing terrible has happened' — coping underestimation).
- If part of the child's fear involves touching the stimulus (e.g., patting a dog/ cat), use guided modelling, whereby you first touch the stimulus while the child watches, and then the child gradually brings their hand alongside your hand to engage with the stimulus.
- Throughout the exposure, encourage the child to continue telling you what they are seeing and noting about the stimulus and their reactions to it. Verbalisation encourages the child to make sense of their experience.
- Take Feelometer ratings after each exposure step.
- Continue with each step until Feelometer ratings of 0–2 (Cool-Warm) are achieved before moving on.
- If set-backs occur, such as the feared outcome eventuating (e.g., a dog growled; the child was unsteady on the ladder; the child's voice trembled when giving a talk in class), focus on the fact that the 'worst has happened' and gather evidence that the child coped. Highlight that although it may have been uncomfortable, the child managed the situation and the risk was not as bad as anticipated. Ensure that exposure continues and

the child remains engaged with the stimulus so they acquire evidence that danger is unlikely and they can cope.

- Exposure is most effective when it is frequent and without lengthy gaps between sessions. It is therefore important that between-session exposure work is organised with parents and children.
- It is also important that exposure opportunities continue well after treatment has been completed. Therefore, practitioners, parents and children should develop additional ACTION Ladders that children work on next as part of relapse prevention and maintenance.

Reviewing ACTION Ladders

Activity Description

After the ACTION Ladder has been devised, it is important the child's progress is reviewed each session. This can be achieved through the use of handouts *IntoAction Home Task Six* and *IntoAction Home Task Seven.*

For Children and Parents Together

It is often helpful to review progress on ACTION ladders with parents and children together. Handout *IntoAction Home Task Six* contains a monitoring sheet for reviewing children's progress on each step on the ACTION Ladder. This monitoring sheet could be assigned as a Home Task or completed together at the start of each session. Practitioners may wish to use the monitoring sheet repeatedly for each step in the ACTION Ladder. Children are instructed to follow the instructions below:

a. Firstly, write down what step you are practising on your ACTION Ladder.
b. For the **Be AWARE step**, write down how you felt, your Anxious Body Signals, and rating on the Feelometer before practising this step on your ACTION Ladder.
c. For the **Keep CALM step**, write down how you kept CALM (e.g. On the Spot Deep Breathing tool).
d. For the **THINK Strong Thoughts step**, write down the Scared Thoughts and Strong Thoughts that you had while practising this step on your ACTION Ladder. You might want to create a Strength Card to help you remember your Strong Thoughts.
e. For the **Get INTO Action step**, write down when you practiced this step on your ACTION Ladder, and your reward.

Using handout *IntoAction Home Task Seven*, which the child can complete at home or practitioners may use in session, ask the child to think about what they did well in that step (e.g., 'I used my breathing to keep calm; I completed the step; I feel Cool on the Feelometer about this step now!')

Then ask children to think about what they could improve during the next step (e.g. 'I will think strong thoughts; I will take my strength card with me'). Parents are encouraged to positively reinforce their child's progress via praise and physical affection (e.g. a hug). Remind children that we want them to practice the ACTION plan strategies on each step of their ACTION Ladder.

Bringing the Steps Together

The major sequence of steps to work through with children up to this point is as follows:

a. Be AWARE of anxiety triggers and anxious body signals
b. Keep CALM by using On the Spot Deep Breathing and Move my Muscles Relaxation
c. Catch scared thoughts
d. Look for thinking themes of overestimation of risk/danger, underestimation of coping, and concern about thinking
e. Identify and THINK Strong Thoughts
f. Use Strength Sayings and Strength Cards to remind children of Strong Thoughts
g. Develop an ACTION Ladder for exposure to feared stimuli
h. Include in-session and between-session exposure exercises in the ACTION Ladder
i. Review progress on ACTION Ladders either as Home Tasks or at the start of each session
j. Ensure exposure therapy in the form of ACTION Ladders continues throughout the remainder of treatment
k. Plan for relapse prevention and maintenance by developing ACTION Ladders to be completed after treatment

References

Waters, A. M., Potter, A., Jamesion, L., Bradley, B. P., & Mogg, K. (2015). Predictors of treatment outcome in anxious children receiving group-based cognitive behavioural therapy: Pre-treatment attention bias for threat and emotional variability during exposure tasks. *Behaviour Change*, *32*, 143–158.

Module 5

O — Use My OPTIONS

Major Activities in this Module

Problem Solving

- Handouts *Options-child-1* to *Options-child-2*
- Handout *Options-parent-1 (A & B)*

Strong Team

- Handout *Options-child-3*

Focus on the Positives

Handouts *KeepCalm-parent-3*; *Options-child-4* to *Options-child-7*

Confident Body Signals (SMILE)

- Handouts *Options-child-8* to *Options-child-9*

Being Confident and Assertive: 3 Ways to Act

- Handout *Options-child-10 (A, B, C)*

Being Confident and Assertive: A 3-step Model

- Handouts *Options-child-11* to *Options-child-12 (A & B)*

Steps for Dealing with Bullying

- Handouts *Options-child-13* to *Options-child-16*

Home Tasks

- Handouts *Options Home Task Eight* and *Options Home Task Nine*

Bringing the Steps Together

Problem Solving

Activity Description

While children are taking ACTION against their anxiety, they are encouraged to use additional coping-oriented OPTIONS to deal with anxious situations. **Use my OPTIONS** is the fifth step in the ACTION Plan. The three OPTIONS that children learn are (1) **Problem Solving**, (2) **Strong Team** (i.e., people who can give them support to keep taking ACTION), and (3) **Focusing on the Positives** and enjoying themselves more.

It is helpful for children to develop good problem solving abilities. This is particularly true for anxious children who often think the ACTION they should take that arises from a Scared Thought is the only option in the situation. These activities aim to teach children that there is always more than one option in any situation, and to weigh up their OPTIONS by thinking about the ACTION they might take if they follow each one. For example, if a child took ACTION that followed from a Scared Thought, they might avoid situations. If they took ACTION that followed from a Strong Thought, they might approach the situation and give it a try.

For Children

Use handout *Options-child-1* to explain the importance of knowing how to solve problems. Explain that children sometimes find it difficult to make decisions when they feel anxious. Reinforce to children that there is always more than one option in any situation, and that the Scared Thought is not likely to be the most helpful option.

Read Dion's story about his scary time, and explain to children how Dion discovered he had two options. The Scared Thought led to unhelpful action for Dion (e.g. missing out on fun at the party). The Strong Thought led to helpful outcomes for Dion (e.g. enjoying himself at the party).Teach children how to weigh up Dion's two options by considering which one leads to the most helpful outcome.

Ask children to think of a scary situation they have experienced recently and complete handout *Options-child-2*. This can be a difficult skill for children so the practitioner assists children through each of the problem solving steps. Encourage children to practice the best option chosen in this activity as a Home Task and this can be reviewed at the next session.

For Parents

Explain that it is important for children to know how to problem solve so they can think of multiple options in a situation, and then choose the best option. Use handout *Options-child-1* to explain the Problem Solving model via Dion's example. Ask parents to think of an anxious situation their child has experienced recently and complete handout *Options-parent-1(A & B)*. It is important that parents know how to effectively problem solve with their child for future scary situations. Parents are also encouraged to use the Problem Solving model to deal with their child's anxious behaviours.

Strong Team

Activity Description

Having a network of supportive people who can help anxious children to cope more effectively in different situations is very important. The goal of this exercise is to develop a Strong Team, or a list of supportive people for each child, who can assist with the implementation of the Take Action strategies.

For Children

Use completed handout *Options-child-3* to explain to children that their second OPTION is a Strong Team. This is a list of supportive people that can assist children with the steps in the ACTION plan. Strong Team members should include adults only, as other children may not have the capabilities to assist the use of the strategies. Strong Team members should not increase Scared Thoughts or encourage unhelpful ACTION (i.e., avoidance). Children are asked to write down the names of at least five supportive people to be on their Strong Team. Children are then asked to write down which situations their Strong Team members can help them with, and how their Strong Team members could best assist them (e.g. 'remind me of the steps in the ACTION plan'). Children are encouraged to ask each person to be on their Strong Team. Role play with children how they will ask their Strong Team members to help them in the best way possible.

For Parents

Use completed handout *Options-child-3* to show parents who their child has nominated as Strong Team members. Discuss the appropriateness of these Strong Team members and make any necessary changes. Parents are encouraged to help their child discuss with these people the situations they might be able to help in, and how they can best assist the child. The practitioner reinforces that Strong Team members are another option for their child to use — they are not the only option (this is to decrease children gaining excessive reassurance from their Strong Team members).

Focus on the Positives

Activity Description

The Take Action program aims to reduce anxiety in children. The program also aims to increase children's self-confidence so that they can enjoy life more. The following activities reinforce the importance of children feeling good and enjoying themselves (referred to as the third OPTION).

For Children

Focus on the Positives

Building on the THINK Strong Thoughts module, Strength Sayings are positive, coping-oriented statements that will help children to feel Strong as they are taking action against anxiety. Give some examples of Strength Sayings such as 'I can do it' and 'I am Strong.' Now that children have had more experience taking action over anxiety through their Action Ladders and by using their Action Plans, use handout *Options-child-4* to assist children to write down more Strength Sayings they could use in anxious situations.

Other possible Strength Sayings to use as prompts are:

- I can Take ACTION.
- I have done it before, I can Take ACTION again.
- I am a Strong person.
- It will not be as bad as I THINK.
- I know how to take ACTION against what is scaring me.
- My fears don't control me.
- Just take one step at a time.
- Relax.
- The worries blow over you and then they are gone.
- Feeling anxious is a signal to use my new skills.
- Keep CALM.
- I am stronger than my fear.
- Every time I face my fear, I get stronger.
- I am Confident.

Keep Being Positive

In the Keep CALM module, parents were encouraged to think about 'feel good' and relaxing activities that their child could start combining into their everyday life. Children are asked to think about how many of these fun 'feel good' activities they are currently participating in.

Use handout *KeepCalm-parent-3* as a guide to discuss with children which 'feel good' and relaxing activities they have been doing each week. Discuss ways to increase the frequency of these 'feel good' relaxing activities. Explain to children that it is important during these activities that they relax and enjoy the positive feelings that are experienced.

Use handout *Options-child-5* to discuss ways to keep being positive. Children are encouraged to use handout *Options-child-6* to think of all the things they do well, and things they like about themselves.

Ask children to read the story on handout *Options-child-7* about Dulcy using the three OPTIONS learnt so far.

For Parents

Use completed handout *Options-child-4* to show parents the Strength Sayings that their child has written down. Ask parents to think about any additional Strength Sayings that could help their child in anxious situations. Parents are encouraged to remind their child of these Strength Sayings and act as a strong role model, by voicing these Strength Sayings out loud to their child.

Children are often involved in structured activities for much of their time at school, and during extra-curricular activities. It is important that children also get to experience spontaneous activities. Use handout *KeepCalm-parent-3* to discuss with parents which 'feel good' and relaxing activities they have incorporated into their child's life. Discuss ways to increase the frequency of these 'feel good' relaxing activities. Explain to parents that it is important during these activities that children enjoy the positive feelings that are experienced. Incorporating some spontaneous, enjoyable activities can be important for anxious children who can sometimes prefer routine and predictability which can interfere with simply having fun.

Use handout *Options-child-5* to discuss with parents the concept of 'being positive'. Parents are shown their child's completed handout *Options-child-6* to see all the things their child has written about what they can do well, and what they like about themselves. Parents are encouraged to discuss these answers with their child and reinforce these positive strengths. Parents are shown the story on completed handout *Options-child-7* to summarise the three OPTIONS learnt so far.

Confident Body Signals (SMILE)

Activity Description

Children who get anxious often find it hard to talk to other people and stand up for themselves, and they might get bullied. Three social skills are taught during the remainder of the Use my OPTIONS step.

Note: When working with younger children aged 4 to 7 years, practitioners should consider the appropriateness of the content in the social skills module, and only use handouts and techniques that are appropriate for the child's age and understanding.

The first social skill is Confident Body Signals or SMILE. This exercise teaches children how to use more confident body signals in social situations with other children and adults.

For Children

Explain the importance of children using good social skills when they are interacting with other children and adults. Use handout *Options-child-8* to explain Confident

Body Signals via the acronym SMILE. Using SMILE will help children look more confident and friendly. Read through each part of SMILE, and check for understanding before moving on to the next part. Then role play SMILE with the child. After SMILE is role played correctly, you can identify and role play the opposite behaviours of SMILE to enhance children's understanding of this important concept:

- For **Stand and face the other person and SMILE**, the opposite would be to look and stand away from the other person;
- For **Make eye contact**, the opposite would be to stare intently or look away from the other person;
- For **Initiate the conversation**, the opposite would be forgetting to use a greeting or introduce yourself, or interrupt the other person;
- For **Listen to the other person**, the opposite would be to talk over the top of the other person;
- For **Enjoy yourself and relax**, the opposite would be to look stressed and feel anxious.

Use handout *Options-child-9* and complete Take Action Task One to brainstorm a list of good conversation topics for children to use when they talk with other children or adults.

Possible conversation topics to use as prompts include:

Sports

School (class work, activities, teachers)

TV shows

Movies

Friends

Books

Games

Family

What happened when I went to a concert / sport / beach...

I'm looking forward to...

Children are then provided with an opportunity to practice Confident Body Signals (SMILE) in a safe environment with you present. For some children who experience social worries, this activity may represent a real challenge as they will be exposed to an anxiety-provoking situation. You should monitor children's reactions to this activity and encourage them to use the steps in the ACTION plan during the task if they feel anxious (e.g. On the Spot Deep Breathing, Strong Thoughts).

Encourage children to choose one of the topics they listed as a good conversation topic. During the first Take Action Task, children get to talk about their chosen topic with the practitioner for up to one minute while they practice SMILE. Once the child has practiced SMILE, swap over the roles so that the practitioner becomes the speaker and the child the listener. Specific feedback should be given to children about their use of each of the SMILE steps. The practitioner should give positive reinforcement for children's effort in using SMILE.

Within a group environment, encourage children to role play the SMILE skills in the same format described above with the other children.

Use handout *Options-child-9* to ask children to discuss how they felt before and after practising SMILE. Ask children how the Confident Body Signals helped them during this task. Encourage children to start practising SMILE with their family and friends. Using Confident Body Signals will help children to be more confident and keep taking action against anxiety.

For Parents

Show parents *Options-child-8* and their child's completed *Options-child-9* to explain Confident Body Signals (SMILE) and the good conversation topics listed. Parents are encouraged to think about what situations their child could practice SMILE in. Parents are also asked to think about how they can prompt their child to use SMILE in these situations.

Being Confident and Assertive: 3 Ways to Act

Activity Description

This exercise teaches children about three different ways to act with other children and adults. Using sea animal characters, children learn about acting in a passive way, aggressive way, and assertive way. This is also an important concept for parents to understand so that they can assist their child to increase their assertiveness in social situations.

For Children

Being able to identify different ways that other children and adults are acting is an important skill for anxious children. Due to their anxiety levels, anxious children often act in a passive way and do not speak up for themselves. Anxious children are often scared about other people's aggressive responses. For example, children often report that their teacher is 'angry' and 'mean' because they yelled at the rest of the class, even though the yelling wasn't directed at the anxious child. Use handout *Options-child-10 (A, B, C)* to read through each of the different ways to act: (1) **passive** e.g. Shy Starfish; (2) **aggressive** e.g. Angry Shark, and (3) **assertive** e.g. Strong Dolphin. It is important that the practitioner checks for understanding after each section (i.e., feelings, body signals, what someone would say, actions). Ask children to provide examples of when they have seen people act this way (e.g. shy student in class; angry teacher in class). The assertive actions (or being the Strong Dolphin) are encouraged as the best way to act, and the next activity teaches children an assertiveness model.

For Parents

Parents are shown completed handouts *Options-child-10 (A, B, C)* to explain the three different ways to act. Ask parents for examples of when their child has acted this way. Parents are encouraged to increase the opportunities for children to practice the assertive way of acting or being the Strong Dolphin.

Being Confident and Assertive: A 3-step Model

Activity Description

An important goal of the Take Action program is for children to become more confident and assertive. These activities teach children a 3-step Assertiveness Model that can be used with other children and adults. Children are also given opportunity to practice the Assertiveness Model with the practitioner. Parents are encouraged to model assertiveness in their own social interactions, and to encourage their children to practice the skill.

For Children

Use handout *Options-child-11* to read Dulcy's story about her swimming cap being taken by her friend. Read Dulcy's responses at each of the three levels of the Assertiveness Model:

1. Tell the other person what you think the problem is.
2. Tell the other person how you feel about the problem, using 'I' statements (e.g. 'I feel upset…')
3. Tell the other person a solution to the problem.

Discuss with children the effectiveness of using assertiveness to solve problems. Children are also encouraged to use the strategies they have learnt in previous modules when they are being assertive (e.g. Keep CALM, THINK Strong Thoughts, SMILE). Children are taught to think about how effective their assertive response was for solving the problem situation. If it worked well, children should congratulate and reward themselves. If the option was not effective, children are encouraged to think of other things they can say next time.

Use handout *Options-child-11* to brainstorm responses for dealing with the two problems described in Take Action Task Two on handout *Options-child-12 (A & B)* assertively:

1. The child is being bossed around, and he/she doesn't want to be bossed around anymore.
2. Another child is trying to copy answers to a Maths test, and he/she doesn't want to give the answers away.

Children are then encouraged to practice the assertive responses with the practitioner (Take Action Task Two). The practitioner provides specific feedback about the child's use of the Assertiveness Model, and prompts the child to use the SMILE skills when speaking.

Within a group environment, encourage children to role play assertive responses in the same format described above with the other children.

For Parents

Parents are shown handouts *Options-child-11* and their child's completed *Options-child-12 (A & B)* to explain the Assertiveness Model, and their child's responses to the two problems. Parents are encouraged to think about what situations their child can practice the Assertiveness Model in. The practitioner encourages parents to act in a confident and assertive way around their child.

Steps for Dealing with Bullying

Activity Description

Knowing strategies for dealing with bullying is very important so that children can become more confident with their peers and cope with more situations. For parents, it is a very stressful experience when their child tells them they are being bullied.

For Children

What is bullying?

It is important that children understand what bullying is so they can identify if they are being bullied by their peers. Use handout *Options-child-13* to explain different ways that children bully. Ask children for examples of when bullying has happened to them or someone else they know.

Use handout *Options-child-13* to discuss different reasons why children bully. Children may have other reasons they have identified about the bullies they know. Discuss with children that bullies are often motivated to bully again if they get a reaction from the child (e.g. the targeted child cries, runs away, or uses physical aggression).

Steps for Dealing with Bullying

Children are encouraged to use the Steps for Dealing with Bullying on handout *Options-child-14.* These strong and confident options will assist children to deal with bullying effectively. The practitioner reads through the three Steps for Dealing with Bullying:

1. Stop what they are doing and practice On The Spot Deep Breathing.

2. Choose a Strong and Confident Option from the circles listed.
3. Decide on the best option and take action.

Children are also encouraged to use the strategies they have learnt in previous modules when they are dealing with bullies (e.g. Keep CALM, THINK Strong Thoughts). Children are taught to think about how effective the option they chose was for the problem situation. If it worked well, children should congratulate and reward themselves. If the option was not effective, children are encouraged to think of other things they can say or do next time.

Use handout *Options-child-15* to read Dion's situation about being bullied by Shawn the shark. Children are encouraged to think about what Dion should do at each step of the Dealing with Bullying model. Children are encouraged to role play their confident responses using the first part of handout *Options-child-16* (Take Action Task Three). Provide specific feedback about the child's use of the Dealing with Bullying steps.

Within a group environment, encourage children to role play the confident responses in the same format described above with the other children.

Discuss how confident children feel in using the Steps for Dealing with Bullying. If the child does not feel confident about practising these skills, the practitioner should role play more hypothetical situations with them in-session. Children are encouraged to keep a diary of the bullying if the Dealing with Bullying strategies do not work. Encourage children to talk to their Strong Team members about the bullying, such as their parents or class teacher.

Story from Dulcy

Read the story on handout *Options-child-16* about Dulcy using the social skills learnt during the Use My Options step. Ask children to write down what they have learnt during the step and discuss their progress.

For Parents

Parents are shown completed handout *Options-child-13* to explain what bullying is, and different reasons why it occurs. Use handout *Options-child-14* to show parents the three Steps for Dealing with Bullying. Parents are encouraged to think about what situations their child may need to practice these dealing with bullying strategies in.

Parents are shown handout *Options-child-16* to discuss how successful their child felt in practising the Steps for Dealing with Bullying, and the Story from Dulcy summarising the Use My OPTIONS step.

Home Tasks

The handouts *Options Home Task Eight* and *Options Home Task Nine* can be used as home tasks if the child needs additional practice of using the 3-step Assertiveness Model and/or the Steps for Dealing with Bullying.

Bringing the Steps Together

The major sequence of steps to work through with children up to this point is as follows:

a. Be AWARE of anxiety triggers and anxious body signals
b. Keep CALM by using On the Spot Deep Breathing and Move my Muscles Relaxation
c. Catch scared thoughts
d. Look for thinking themes of overestimation of risk/danger, underestimation of coping, and concern about thinking
e. Identify Strong Thoughts
f. Use Strength Sayings and Strength Cards to remind children of Strong Thoughts
g. Develop an ACTION Ladder for exposure to feared stimuli, and start exposure sessions
h. Review progress on ACTION Ladders either as Home Tasks or at the start of each session
i. Ensure exposure therapy in the form of ACTION Ladders continues throughout the remainder of treatment
j. Plan for relapse prevention and maintenance by developing ACTION Ladders to be completed after treatment
k. Use the Problem Solving model in anxious situations
l. Develop a Strong Team and ask the listed people to assist in anxious situations
m. Use Strength Sayings and Keep Being Positive strategies
n. Use Confident Body Signals (SMILE) in social situations with other children and adults
o. Use the three-step model to being Confident and Assertive in problem situations
p. Use the steps for Dealing with Bullying if needed in problem situations

Module 6

N — NEVER Stop Taking Action

Major activities in this Module

Reviewing the Six Steps in the ACTION Plan

- Handouts *NeverStop-child-1* to *NeverStop-child-2B*

Reviewing Progress

Handouts *NeverStop-child-3* to *NeverStop-child-4*

Looking Ahead to Other Scary Situations

Handout *NeverStop-child-5* to *NeverStop-child-6*

Take Action Bookmark and Story from Dulcy and Dion

Handout *NeverStop-child-7* to *NeverStop-child-8*

Bringing the steps together

Reviewing the Six Steps in the Action Plan

Activity Description

The main goal in this activity is to ensure children and parents understand (1) the importance of continued use of the strategies learnt through the Take Action program and (2) of ongoing exposure to feared stimuli and situations. As outlined in earlier modules, avoidance plays a major role in the continuation of anxiety. Ongoing exposure to fear stimuli, in conjunction with the use of strategies taught through the program, help children to manage anxiety and remain calm and happy over time.

For Children and Parents Together

Use handout *NeverStop-child-1* to review the six steps in the ACTION Plan. Ask children to tell you what they remember about each step and the main strategies they can use from each one. Ask parents what they can do at each step to assist their child in the implementation of these strategies.

To further highlight the major strategies in each step of the ACTION Plan, ask the child to read aloud the story of a child who is afraid of going to school and how the ACTION Plan and their ACTION Ladder can help (handout *NeverStop-child-2 (A & B)*).

Reviewing Progress

Activity Description

Reviewing progress from the start to the end of the program is a helpful way for children and parents to see that continued engagement in taking action over anxiety leads to good outcomes. This can set the basis for motivating children and parents to continue with this approach as they plan for the future and potential challenges that might arise.

For Children and Parents Together

Using handout *NeverStop-child-3*, ask children to write words or draw pictures about how they felt before they started the Take Action program. Then using the upper panel in handout *NeverStop-child-4*, ask children to write words or draw pictures about how they feel now they have completed the Take Action program. Highlight to children and parents the change that has taken place from before to after the program.

Using the lower panel in handout *NeverStop-child-4*, write words or draw pictures about 2–3 positive things you as the practitioner have noted about the child's progress during the program. It is helpful to share these comments with children and parents and to encourage them to continue using these skills and strong behaviours in the future.

Looking Ahead to Other Scary Situations

Activity Description

Planning for events in the future that might be anxiety-provoking is helpful for preventing relapse, or the return of anxiety. This means that when a potentially anxiety-provoking situation is approaching (e.g., returning to school after the holidays; attending a birthday party or sleep-over), children may be reminded of the steps in their ACTION Plan and an ACTION Ladder could be implemented to encourage exposure to situations relevant to the upcoming event. For a fear of returning to school, a potential ACTION Ladder could be: step (1) getting school books together; (2) looking on the school website for recent news and events; (3) looking at class photos for children who will be in his/her class; (4) rehearsing school drop-off routine; (5) play-dates with children in his/her class.

For Children and Parents Together

Use handout *NeverStop-child-5* to encourage children and parents to identify times in the future that might be challenging or scary. Work through the activities to identify strategies at each step of the ACTION plan that will help when dealing with these future scary times. Encourage children and parents to develop an ACTION

Ladder (via handout *NeverStop-child-6*) to work towards in relation to at least one of these scary situations.

Take Action Bookmark and Story from Dulcy and Dion

Activity Description

It is helpful for children to have a reminder tool of the six steps in their ACTION plan which they can access easily. This could be in the form of a Bookmark they create in session using cardboard, pens and stickers, or a reminder card they can place on their mirror or beside their bed.

For Children and Parents Together

Work with children and parents to create the bookmark or reminder card. Generate options for where it would be best to display the card so the child will see it often. This should be somewhere parents are familiar with as well, so they can encourage children to look at the bookmark or reminder card if they notice signs of anxiety developing or a potentially anxiety-provoking situation is coming up.

Finally, ask children to read the final story from Dulcy and Dion which summarises the main points of the Never Stop Taking Action step (handout *NeverStop-child-7*). Ask children what they learnt during this step.

The practitioner presents children with the Certificate for completing the Take Action program (handout *NeverStop-child-8*). Children and parents are congratulated on their hard work and effort during the program.

Bringing the Steps Together

The major sequence of steps to work through with children up to this point is as follows:

a. Be AWARE of anxiety triggers and anxious body signals
b. Keep CALM by using On the Spot Deep Breathing and Move My Muscles Relaxation
c. Catch scared thoughts
d. Look for thinking themes of overestimation of risk/danger, underestimation of coping, and concern about thinking
e. Identify Strong Thoughts
f. Use Strength Sayings and Strength Cards to remind children of Strong Thoughts
g. Ensure exposure therapy in the form of ACTION Ladders continues throughout the remainder of treatment
h. Plan for relapse prevention and maintenance by developing ACTION Ladders to be completed after treatment

i. Use the Problem Solving model in anxious situations
j. Develop a Strong Team and ask the listed people to assist in anxious situations
k. Use Strength Sayings and Keep Being Positive strategies
l. Use Confident Body Signals (SMILE) in social situations with other children and adults
m. Use the three-step model to being Confident and Assertive in problem situations
n. Use the steps for Dealing with Bullying if needed in problem situations
o. Keep the Take ACTION Bookmark and all handouts somewhere accessible so that the six steps in the ACTION plan can be continually reviewed following treatment
p. Develop additional ACTION Ladders to encourage exposure to future scary situations

Considerations when Working with Children Who have Comorbid Conditions

In this section of the Practitioner Guide, we share some of our experience in working with children diagnosed with commonly associated comorbid conditions. Often children presenting to our clinic under a paediatrician or psychiatrist referral, have been diagnosed with anxiety disorder/s comorbid with other developmental conditions. This section does not set out to cover a prescriptive treatment for any of these conditions listed.

Working with Children Diagnosed with an ASD

In our experience with the Take Action program, children diagnosed with an Autistic Spectrum Disorder (ASD) can understand the concepts and learn the strategies well. In our clinic, more time is taken with the child to develop their understanding of different emotions, with particular emphasis on identifying facial expressions. Younger children like the Feelings sea animal characters and they have been able to use these characters to successfully identify different emotions in others. For example, a boy diagnosed with an Autistic Spectrum Disorder identified his teacher as being 'angry like Shawn the Shark' when she was yelling at the class. This helped the boy to understand that the teacher was not yelling at him and his anxiety was reduced in the classroom. It is often important to discuss other emotions in more depth as well, such as anger and sadness. Using the Feelometer to rate the intensity of anger and sadness works successfully for ASD children. Additional strategies for reducing anger or sadness may be needed (e.g. safe tension release activities), and this is where the practitioner's conceptualisation after the assessment process is important.

We have found that more emphasis is needed on the cognitive strategies (THINK Strong Thoughts step) to improve ASD children's ability to think flexibly. The Strength Cards are a useful tool for children to identify their anxious thoughts, and improve their coping-oriented Strong Thoughts. The cards can then be taken to the anxious situation and this has helped many children in the school environment.

The entire Use my OPTIONS step is very important to cover in depth with children diagnosed with ASD. The Problem Solving model can also be adapted for use in angry situations. Each of the social skills learnt in this step are vital to reinforce with these children who often have difficulty with confident non-verbal behaviour, being assertive, and knowing how to deal with bullying effectively. Extensive role playing of these social skills with the practitioner is useful. However, we also encourage parents to regularly role play the social skills with their child using real-life or hypothetical situations.

Working with Children Diagnosed with ADHD

As children diagnosed with Attention-Deficit/Hyperactivity Disorder (ADHD) often have social skills deficits, the Use my OPTIONS step is vitally important to cover in depth. The Problem Solving model is useful for children with ADHD, however it is beneficial to add an initial step of getting children to STOP and use their On the Spot Deep Breathing when a problem has been identified. Children can then progress through the same steps of looking at the various OPTIONS they have in the situation, before choosing the best option. If children with a comorbid diagnosis of ADHD do not STOP first, their problem solving abilities may be impaired. The social skills of assertiveness and dealing with bullying strategies are often useful for these children. Role playing these social skills with the practitioner, in addition to real-practice with their parents and/or peers is useful.

Working with Children Diagnosed with Speech and Language Problems

We have worked with many children diagnosed with comorbid speech and language problems. The practitioner may need to determine whether the child can engage with the level of language used in some of the handouts, particularly in the THINK Strong Thoughts step. However, children often enjoy the visual handouts with their friendly interesting cartoons and engaging stories. The Feelings sea animal characters have been extremely useful to assist younger children in understanding different emotions. We encourage all family members to discuss the sea animal characters at home and build that association with the different emotions.

Strength cards have been useful as children can draw pictures and use simple language, but the child is still using Strong thoughts to assist them in anxious situations. Role plays with the practitioner and parents are integral for children so that the concepts are well understood.

Trouble Shooting

In our work with the Take Action program, children and parents have shared the following concerns for which we have provided the tips below.

'We've done that before and it didn't work'

If children have attended another service or engaged in CBT previously, they might say that they have learnt the strategies before and they did not work to reduce their anxiety. Parents can also be reluctant to try different strategies to what they have been shown in the past. It is important that you explain your experience in working with anxious children, and the effectiveness of the Take Action program within individual and group formats. Ask the child and parent what they have learnt before and look at any previous handouts they have received. Explain to children and parents that they will be participating in a manualised treatment program and describe the ACTION plan, comparing the similarities or differences to the previous treatment they have completed. Your confidence and belief in the program will assist children and parents to feel more comfortable and hopeful that this program will work for them. Reassure children and parents that if any of the strategies are not useful during the program, that you can brainstorm different ways to assist the child's anxiety problems.

Not Completing Home Tasks

Much of the Take Action program skills are learnt in session with the practitioner. However, it is crucial that the child is practising the ACTION plan strategies at home and in other anxious situations for their anxiety to be significantly reduced. Discuss with children and parents the obstacles to completing homework, and problem solve some solutions. For example, a child who is not practising their On the Spot Deep Breathing could be reminded that the breathing technique is to be used 'On the Spot' in any situation in which they feel anxious. You could then role play some hypothetical situations with the child and show them how they could use their Deep Breathing successfully. Increasing the strength of rewards may also assist the child's compliance with the home tasks.

'My strategies aren't working' or 'Progress is slow'

When children report that their strategies aren't working in reducing their anxiety, parents often feel that their progress is slow. Anxiety can be very distressing for children and parents, and when they present for treatment, they often want to see reductions in anxiety very quickly. While this is understandable, it is important to continue reviewing the child's progress and where they are up to in the ACTION plan. Reinforce the importance of practising the strategies learnt in all anxious situations. The more children practice the ACTION plan strategies, the sooner the anxiety will subside.

'I feel better now, can I stop treatment?'

It is very important that children are provided with materials from the entire Take Action program. Anxiety waxes and wanes in general during childhood so a significant reduction in the first few weeks of treatment indicates the strategies are working, but it is not a good time to finish treatment. This is where the initial assessment and conceptualisation is important so that the practitioner can review this if the child wants to complete treatment early. Follow-up (booster) sessions are recommended at one month, three months and six month intervals. If a child or parent wants to end treatment early, the practitioner could schedule a booster session for the future to monitor the child's progress and maintenance of treatment gains.

Appendix A
Child Handouts

Module 1.1

Introduction

Module 1.2

A — Be Aware

Module 2

C — Keep Calm

Module 3

T — Strong Thoughts

Module 4

I — Into Action

Module 5

O — Options

Module 6

N — Never Stop

Take Action

Introduction 1

The Interview Exercise

We are going to get to know each other, as well as learn about how the Take Action program can help you. Your first activity is to find out the answers to the questions below.

Ask your new friend sitting beside you the following questions and write down their answers.

1. What is your friend's full name?

   ____

2. What is your friend's favourite TV show?

   ____

3. What is your friend's favourite book to read?

   ____

4. What is your friend's favourite computer game?

   ____

5. What grade is your friend in at school?

   ____

6. How many brothers and sisters does your friend have?

   ____

Congratulations! You have completed your first activity in the Take Action program!

A Step One

I can be AWARE of my Anxious Feelings and Body Signals.

WELCOME to the Take Action program!

You will learn how to take ACTION against your fears and worries so that you can enjoy things more and be happier!

Dulcy and Dion, your two new dolphin friends, will be learning to take ACTION with you.

Dulcy and Dion both think that it is normal to feel scared or worried when you are in danger. Everyone feels scared or worried at some time — it is a normal part of life.

Sometimes we get scared when there is NO real danger.

Situations like being in the dark, or being away from Mum or Dad, or making new friends might seem scary but they are not dangerous.

You can learn to feel better about anything that scares or worries you by taking ACTION.

Take Action

Be Aware
Child 2A

Dion knows that children and adults get scared or worried sometimes for different reasons, but he has a question for you:

Activity
What is Anxiety?

Write down all the words you can think of that are used to describe anxiety on the lines below:

____

____

____

____

____

____

____

____

Now you know what anxiety means, it is time to learn about your ACTION Plan.

Be Aware
Child 2B

Take Action

You will learn the six steps in the ACTION plan during the Take Action program. Each step will help you to take action against anxiety. By the end of the program, you will have an ACTION plan to keep and use in the future.

A

Step One:
I can be **AWARE** of my Anxious Feelings and Body Signals.

C

Step Two:
I can keep **CALM** by doing On the Spot Deep Breathing and Move my Muscles Relaxation.

T

Step Three:
I can **THINK** Strong Thoughts.

I

Step Four:
I can get **INTO** Action by climbing the steps of my Action Ladder and rewarding myself.

O

Step Five:
I can use my **OPTIONS** including Problem Solving, Strong Team, and to Focus on the Positives. I can use my social skills to be more Strong, Confident and Assertive, and Deal with Bullies.

N

Step Six:
I will **NEVER** stop taking action against anxiety.

You are learning to take action against anxiety so you can enjoy things more and be happy!

Take Action

Be Aware
Child 3

Now we have worked out how to take ACTION together, Dulcy and Dion would like to tell you a story about themselves.

Dulcy and Dion the dolphins are really good friends. Dulcy and Dion are scared about learning to swim but they don't want to miss out on all the fun.

Dulcy is scared of the swimming teacher Mrs Seahorse because she has a loud voice. Dulcy is afraid Mrs Seahorse will think she is a bad swimmer and yell at her.

Dion is scared of swimming in the deep end.

But Dulcy says to herself: "Mrs Seahorse has a loud voice but she knows I am a beginner. I will try my best and the swimming lesson will be fun."

Dion says to himself: "I have swum in the deep end before on holidays and nothing bad happened to me. I can do it again."

Dulcy and Dion were scared about learning to swim at first, but they took ACTION against their fears by thinking Strong thoughts. They found out that they could have fun at their swimming lesson.

Activity
My Take ACTION Goals

Read the Worry Wall below and think about when you feel anxious.

Being away from mum or dad or home	Of certain things e.g. darkness, animals	In situations with other people e.g. doing a speech
School e.g. grades, homework, assignments	Performance e.g. being good in things like sports	Social e.g. making friends, what others think of you
Little things e.g. what happened in the past	Perfectionism e.g. never making mistakes	Health of yourself or others
Family e.g. money worries	Things going on in the world e.g. war, natural disasters	Other worries

Write down when you feel anxious on the lines below.

I feel extremely anxious when:

____

I feel a lot of anxiety when:

____

I feel a little bit of anxiety when:

____

I feel calm and relaxed when:

____

From the lists above, think about the worries or fears that you would like to take ACTION against. Write your Take ACTION goals on the lines below:

____

____

Take Action

Be Aware
Child 5

Be AWARE of Anxious Feelings

A great way to work out how you are feeling in different situations is the **Feelometer**.

The **Feelometer** is just like a thermometer that can tell your temperature.

You can use the **Feelometer** to know how anxious you are feeling at different times.

Look at the **Feelometer** below:

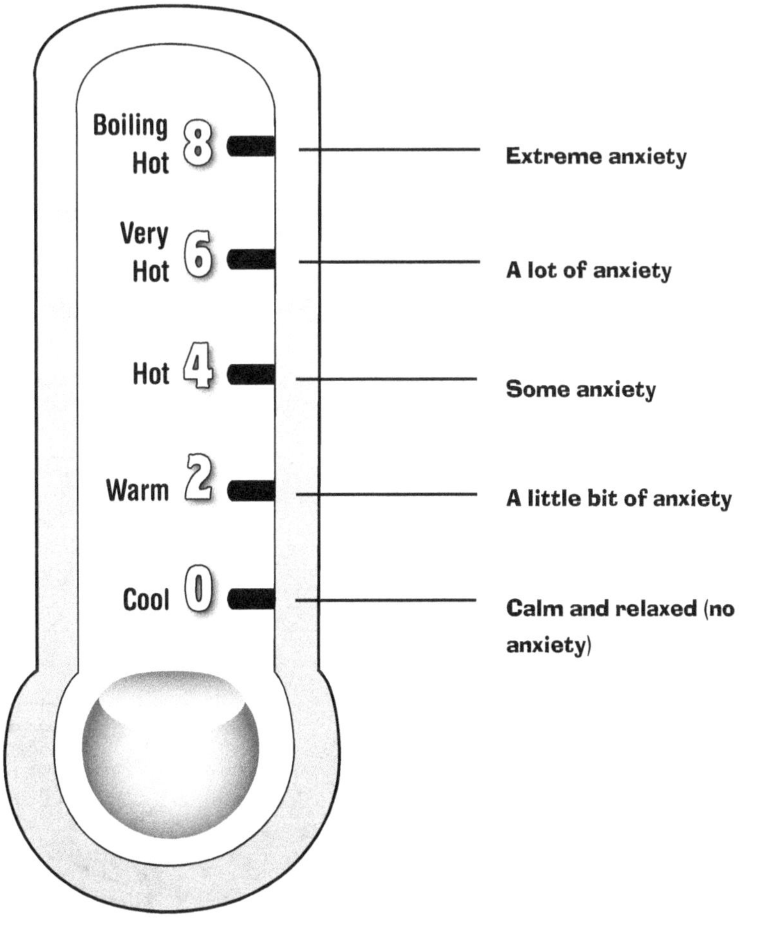

Activity
Using the Feelometer

If you rated your anxiety levels as ***cool*** on the Feelometer, you would feel calm and relaxed (no anxiety at all). Write down a time when you have felt **calm and relaxed**:

____

____

If you rated your anxiety levels as ***warm*** on the Feelometer, you would be feeling a little bit of anxiety. Write down a time when you have felt **a little bit of anxiety**:

____

____

If you rated your anxiety levels as ***hot*** on the Feelometer, you would be feeling some anxiety. Write down a time when you have felt **some anxiety**:

____

____

If you rated your anxiety levels as ***very hot*** on the Feelometer, you would be feeling a lot of anxiety. Write down a time when you have felt **a lot of anxiety**:

____

____

If you rated your anxiety levels as ***boiling hot*** on the Feelometer, you would be feeling extreme anxiety. Write down a time when you have felt **extreme anxiety**:

____

____

You can use the Feelometer to tell you how anxious you are feeling. To be AWARE of your anxious feelings and the times when you need to Take ACTION is part of the first step in the ACTION plan.

Take Action

Be Aware
Child 7

Be AWARE: Anxiety is a Good Alarm and a False Alarm

Anxiety is a common emotion that we all experience. Everyone feels scared or worried at some time — it is a normal part of life. Anxiety is a signal that there is danger. In the caveman days, it was very important for cavemen to get scared if they saw a sabre-tooth tiger so they could either fight the tiger or run away to safety.

Real DANGER!

As soon as the caveman saw the sabre-tooth tiger, the caveman's brain would send messages of danger to his body, making his heart beat fast and his hands cold. He might also sweat a lot and get butterflies in his stomach. These changes in his body would help him to take ACTION and survive because he could either fight the tiger if he had to, or run away from the tiger to safety.

Children and adults get the same changes in their bodies today. If we have to fight or escape from a dangerous situation, our bodies change to help us to be strong and take ACTION. This is when anxiety is helpful! It is normal to feel scared when you are in real danger — just like the caveman.

Sometimes we have 'false alarms' and we feel scared in our bodies when there is no real danger. When there is a 'false alarm', we feel ***Boiling Hot*** on the Feelometer when we should feel ***Cool*** (this is happening to the boy below). You can be AWARE of these 'false alarms', by working out how anxious you feel on the Feelometer.

False ALARM

Be Aware
Child 8

Take Action

Be AWARE of Anxious Body Signals

Dulcy has listened to her body and she has noticed these Anxious Body Signals (see them below). The hotter Dulcy feels on the Feelometer, the more Anxious Body Signals she has.

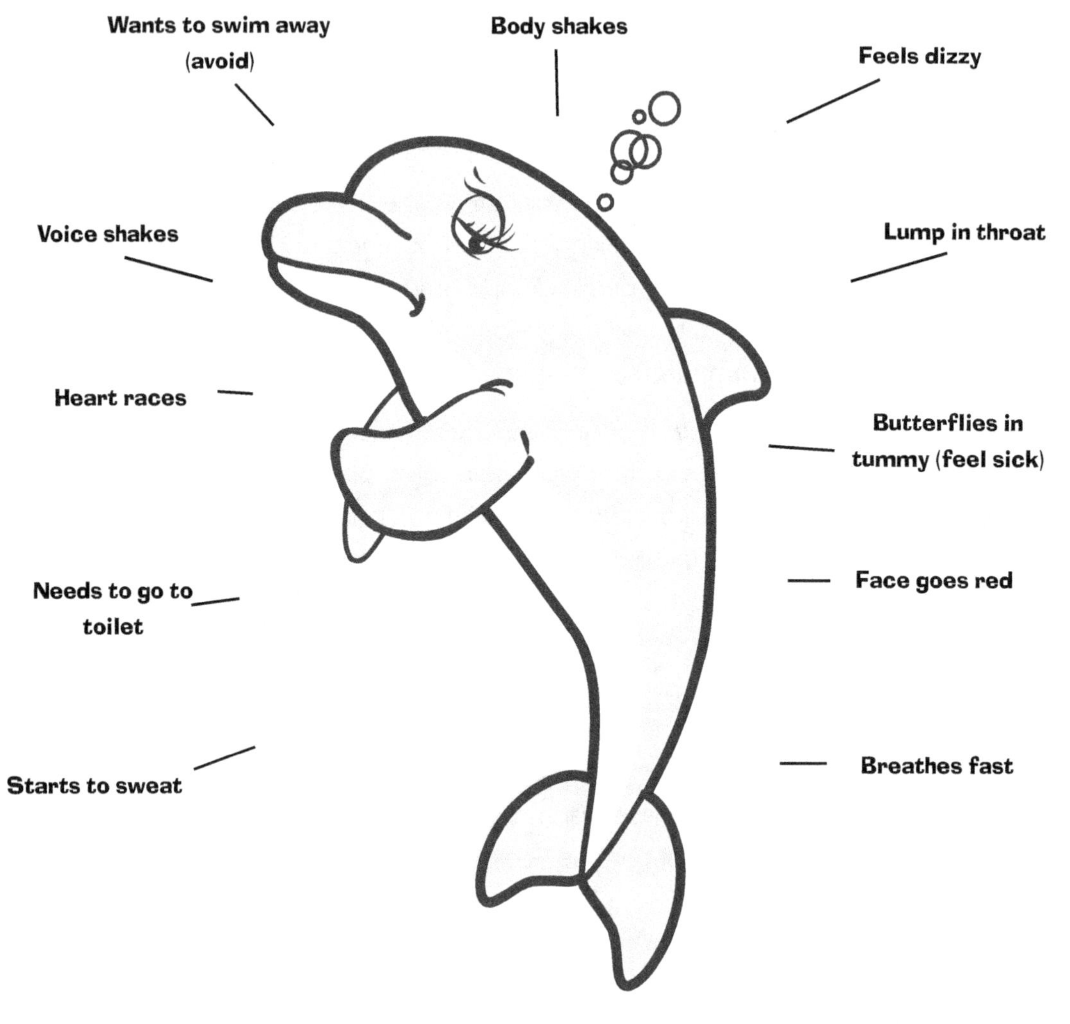

Take Action

Activity

Be AWARE of Your Anxious Body Signals

Work out which Anxious Body Signals you get when you feel anxious.

Think of a time when you felt anxious and write it down:

____

Rate your Feelings on the Feelometer: ________________________

Colour in the Anxious Body Signals shown below that you had when you felt anxious.

Add in any other Anxious Body Signals that are not listed.

Be Aware
Child 10

Take Action

Activity
Be AWARE of Feelings on Faces

Another way you can be AWARE of false alarms is by the look on other people's faces. If you feel anxious but other people look calm or happy, it could be a false alarm. Look at the faces below and write down the correct feeling for each one.

What feeling/s is this face showing?

____

What feeling/s is this face showing?

____

What feeling/s is this face showing?

____

What feeling/s is this face showing?

____

Knowing how you are feeling helps you go from Hot to Cool on the Feelometer, and 'stops false alarms'.

Whenever you feel anxious, Stop, Look at other people's faces for clues about how to feel, and Learn from your Anxious Body Signals so you can take ACTION.

Take Action

Be Aware
Child 11A

Be AWARE of Different Feelings

Just like there are lots of different sea animals living in the ocean, there are lots of different feelings that we can feel.

This is Dulcy the dolphin

Dulcy likes to dive in and out of the water. Dulcy feels HAPPY. She feels so happy when she swims in and out of the water with her friends. Sometimes we feel happy like Dulcy the dolphin.

This is Claire the clam

Claire stays inside her shell. She feels SCARED. She does not want to leave her shell in case she gets eaten. Sometimes we feel scared like Claire the clam.

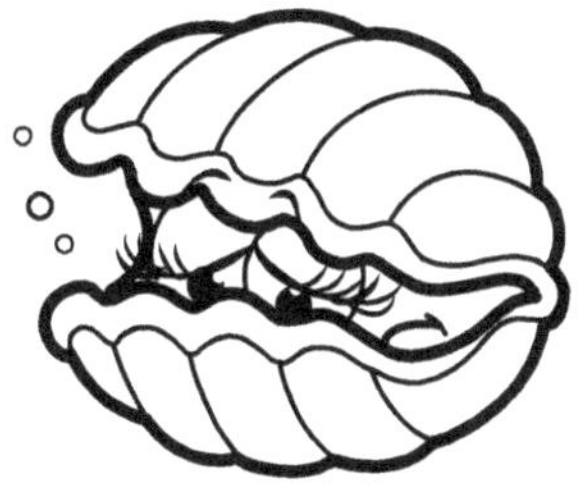

This is Wendy the whale

Wendy swims through the sea all on her own. Wendy feels SAD. She sings a sad whale song that you can hear under the sea. Sometimes we feel sad like Wendy the whale.

Be Aware
Child 11B

Take Action

This is Shawn the shark

Shawn does not like it when he gets caught in a shark net. Shawn feels ANGRY. He yells and hits the shark net with his fins. Sometimes we feel angry like Shawn the shark.

This is Tommy the turtle

Tommy surfs the current in the sea. Tommy feels CALM. Tommy feels so cool when he surfs with his friends. Sometimes we feel calm like Tommy the turtle.

Wendy feels SAD

Dulcy feels HAPPY

Tommy feels CALM

Shawn feels ANGRY

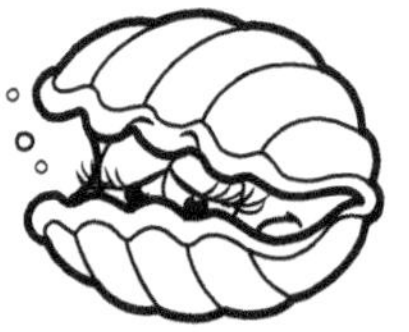

Claire feels SCARED

Take Action

Be Aware
Child 12

Activity
Be AWARE of Your Feelings

Read the story about Olivia and answer the questions below.

Olivia was having lots of fun playing outside in her backyard. She had been out there nearly all day. Then, her mum said that she was going to the shops and she would be back in 20 minutes. Olivia does not like her mum going anywhere without her.

How do you think Olivia felt when her mum said she was going to the shops?

____

Circle the face which matches Olivia's feeling:

Write down a time when you have felt like Olivia:

____

Rate your Feelings on the Feelometer:

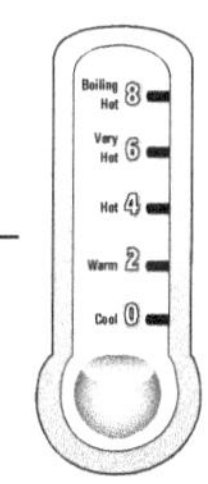

____

What did you say or do when you felt like Olivia?

____

Did you do anything to help yourself feel better during this time?

____

____

Activity
Be AWARE of Your Feelings

Read the story about Paul and answer the questions below.

Paul just got an ice-cream from the shop. It is his favourite type of ice-cream – raspberry! Yummy!

How do you think Paul felt when he got his ice-cream?

____

Circle the face which matches Paul's feeling:

Write down a time when you have felt like Paul:

____

Rate your Feelings on the Feelometer:

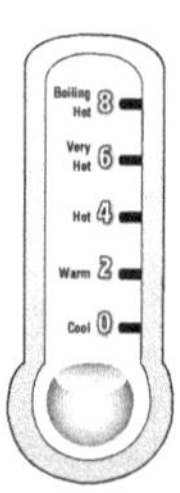

____

What did you say or do when you felt like Paul?

____

____

____

A Story from Dulcy

Dulcy thinks that being more aware in anxious situations is a great idea. Remember how Dulcy felt scared about her teacher Mrs Seahorse's loud voice when she was going to her swimming lesson?

In the future, Dulcy can be more aware by scanning her body to see if there have been any changes, like a fast beating heart. Dulcy can then decide whether it is a dangerous situation, or whether her body has set off a 'false alarm'. Dulcy can also scan the faces of the other sea animals around her to see how they are feeling about the swimming lesson. She can use the Feelometer to work out how anxious she is feeling.

Dulcy is going to take ACTION at her next swimming lesson, and she thinks it will be fun and safe.

Activity

Dulcy would like to ask you what you have learnt during the Be AWARE step.

Write down your answers on the lines below.

____

____

____

____

____

This page is intentionally blank.

Take Action

Keep Calm
Child 1

C Step Two

I can keep CALM by doing On the Spot Deep Breathing and Move My Muscles Relaxation.

The first way to keep CALM is to practise On the Spot Deep Breathing.

On the Spot Deep Breathing can be used whenever you feel anxious and no one has to know you are doing it. That's why it's called "on the spot" deep breathing! Deep breathing helps you to stay CALM and not let your Anxious Body Signals bother you.

Let's see how it works:

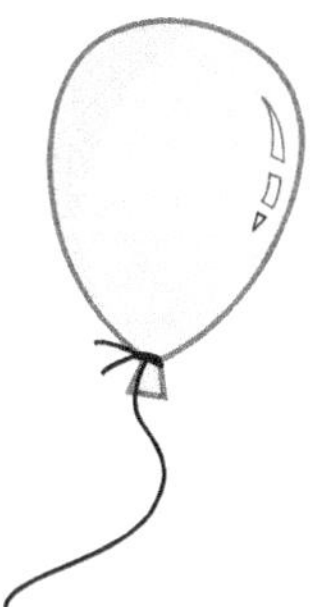

1. Place one hand on your stomach and one hand on your chest. Imagine you have a balloon in your stomach and you want to blow it up really big. This means you have to push the air you breathe in all the way down into your stomach.
2. Slowly breathe in through your nose, counting to 3 and "blow up the balloon" in your stomach (make it big like the balloon above). Your chest should not move, only your stomach. Watch to see that only your hand on your stomach goes up as you "fill the balloon with air".
3. Hold your breath while you keep the balloon filled with air and say **Relax** to yourself.
4. Slowly breathe out through your nose counting to 3. The balloon in your stomach will get smaller when you breathe out, and the hand on your stomach should go down.
5. Hold your breath and say **Relax** to yourself.

Each time you practise your Breathing blow the balloon UP and DOWN in your stomach at least 5 times.

Activity
Using On the Spot Deep Breathing

Write down when you could use On the Spot Deep Breathing to keep CALM on the lines below:

____

____

Keep Calm
Child 2

Take Action

The second way to keep CALM is to practise Move My Muscles Relaxation.

Relaxation works really well in getting rid of the tightness in your muscles. In this relaxation exercise, you tense and then relax muscles from your face to your feet.

Let's see how it works:

1. **FACE:** Screw up your face (including your nose and eyes) and count to 3. Pretend that you have just smelt something really bad. Then say **Relax** to yourself and relax your face.
2. **SHOULDERS:** Shrug your shoulders upwards — try to make them touch your ears — and count to 3. Then say **Relax** to yourself and drop your shoulders down again.
3. **HANDS:** Squeeze your fingers together, like you are squeezing a ball and count to 3. Then say **Relax** to yourself and let your fingers open up.
4. **STOMACH:** Pull your stomach in and pretend you are trying to squeeze through a very small gap. Count to 3. Then say **Relax** to yourself and push your stomach out again.
5. **LEGS:** Make your legs really straight and tighten all the muscles in your legs. Count to 3. Then say **Relax** to yourself and make your legs all floppy (like a rag doll).
6. **FEET:** Clench and point your toes towards the floor. Count to 3. Then say **Relax** to yourself, roll your feet around in circles, and relax your toes

Activity
Move My Muscles Relaxation

Write down when you could use Move My Muscles Relaxation to keep CALM:

____

____

Take Action

Keep Calm
Child 3A

Move My Muscles Relaxation Cards

1. FACE:

Screw up your face (including your nose and eyes) and count to 3. Pretend that you have just smelt something really bad. Then say **Relax** to yourself and relax your face.

2. SHOULDERS:

Shrug your shoulders upwards — try to make them touch your ears — and count to 3. Then say **Relax** to yourself and drop your shoulders down again.

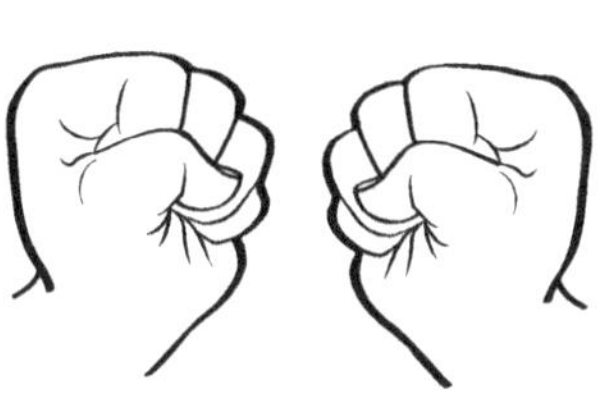

3. HANDS:

Squeeze your fingers together, like you are squeezing a ball and count to 3. Then say **Relax** to yourself and let your fingers open up.

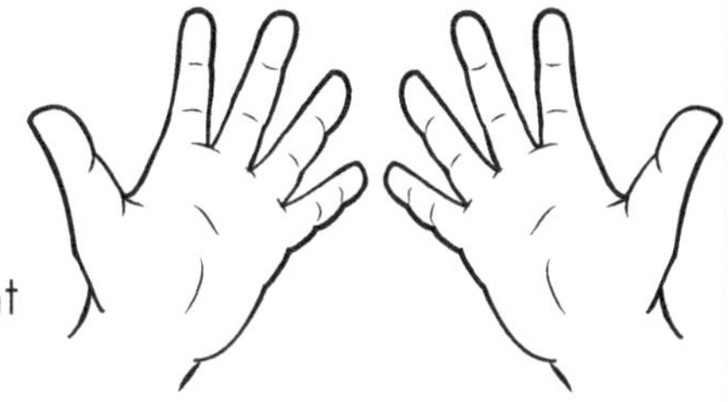

Keep Calm
Child 3B

4. STOMACH:

Pull your stomach in and pretend you are trying to squeeze through a very small gap. Count to 3. Then say **Relax** to yourself and push your stomach out again.

5. LEGS:

Make your legs really straight and tighten all the muscles in your legs. Count to 3. Then say **Relax** to yourself and make your legs all floppy (like a rag doll).

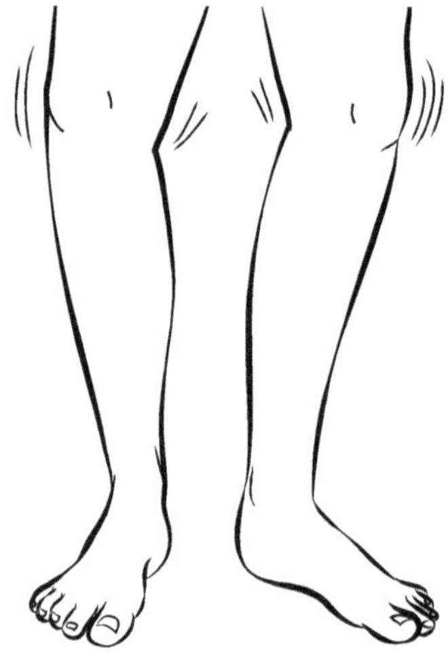

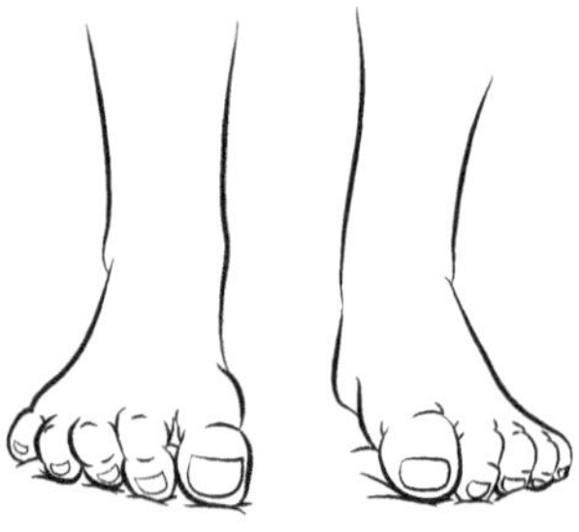

6. FEET:

Clench and point your toes towards the floor. Count to 3. Then say **Relax** to yourself, roll your feet around in circles, and unclench your toes.

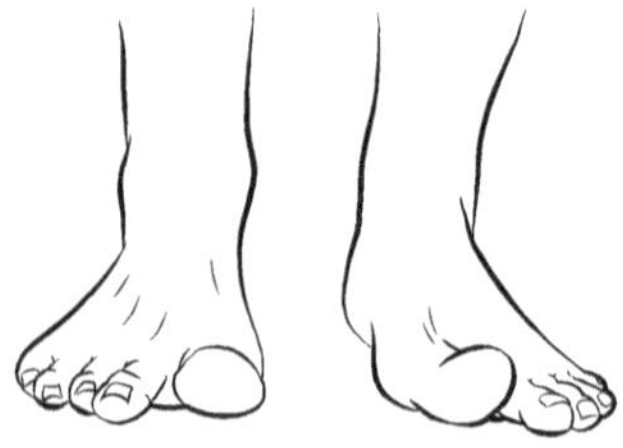

Take Action

Keep Calm
Child 4

Congratulations! You have learnt two ways to keep CALM. Practise your On the Spot Deep Breathing and Muscle Relaxation whenever you are AWARE of feeling anxious!

A Story from Dion

Dion can see that you have learnt about how to be AWARE of your Anxious Body Signals and different feelings shown on our faces. You can now use the Feelometer to help work out how anxious you are feeling. You also learnt about ways to keep CALM. Dion liked the On the Spot Deep Breathing and he is going to use this to help keep himself CALM in scary situations. It is also a good idea to keep your muscles relaxed so it is easier to take ACTION against anxiety. Dion thinks that learning how to keep CALM is like learning how to play a new computer game. If you practise every day, you will get really good at it.

Activity

Dion would like to ask you what you have learnt during the Keep CALM step.

Write down your answers on the lines below:

____

____

____

Take Action

Activity
Planning for your Home Task

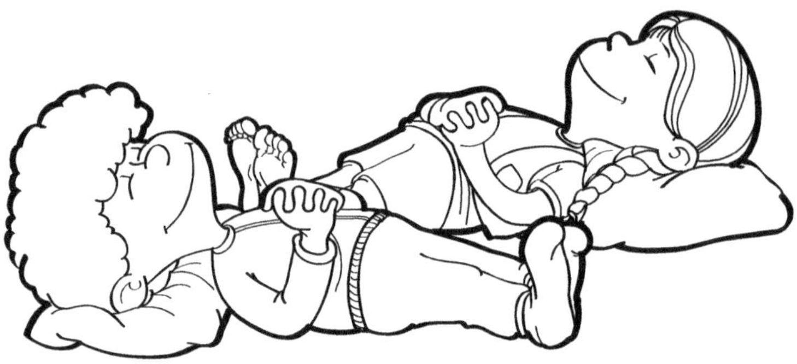

Your Home Task is to practise On the Spot Deep Breathing and Move My Muscles Relaxation every day. First let's do some planning so your Home Task is easy to finish.

1. Circle what time each day you will practise On the Spot Deep Breathing (you can circle more than one time):

   Morning   During the day   Afternoon   Night Time

2. Circle what time you will practise Move My Muscles Relaxation:

   Morning   During the day   Afternoon   Night Time

3. Think about what might stop you from doing your Breathing and Relaxation practice. Write down the things that might stop you from doing your Breathing and Relaxation on the lines below:

   ____

   ____

   ____

4. Write down how you can make sure that you practise your Breathing and Relaxation on the lines below:

   ____

   ____

   ____

Take Action

Thoughts
Child 1

T Step Three

I can THINK Strong Thoughts

Do you know that your thoughts are different to your feelings?

Thoughts come from inside your head. As Dulcy was going to school, she had two different thoughts:

We have talked about feelings like happy, angry, sad and anxious. Thoughts have a very powerful effect on Feelings and what you Do:

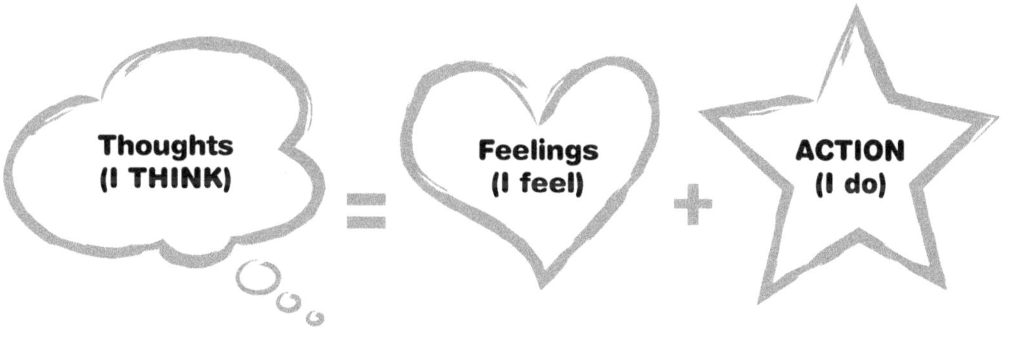

The way you THINK can change how you feel and what you do because your thoughts always come first!

Thoughts
Child 2

Activity
It's all about how we THINK

Let's learn more about thoughts and how they can change the way you feel and what you do.

Three animals are going to their first swimming lesson in the ocean. The animals are good at swimming in the pool, but this is the first time they have swum in the ocean. Each animal thinks about swimming in the ocean in a different way. Write down the feeling you THINK each animal would have because of their thoughts.

How might Dianne the Duck be feeling?

____

How might Freddie the Fish be feeling?

____

How might Sammy the Starfish be feeling?

____

Take Action

Thoughts
Child 3

Activity
What you THINK is what you feel and do

THINK of a time when you felt anxious like Dianne the Duck.
Write your answers on the lines below:

I felt anxious when ______________________________

Rate your Feelings on the Feelometer: ______________________________

What did you THINK about when you felt anxious? ______________________________

What did you DO when you felt anxious? ______________________________

____

THINK of a time when you felt angry like Freddie the Fish.
Write your answers on the lines below:

I felt angry when ______________________________

Rate your Feelings on the Feelometer: ______________________________

What did you THINK about when you felt angry? ______________________________

What did you DO when you felt angry? ______________________________

____

THINK of a time when you felt happy like Sammy the Starfish.
Write your answers on the lines below:

I felt happy when ______________________________

Rate your Feelings on the Feelometer: ______________________________

What did you THINK about when you felt happy? ______________________________

What did you DO when you felt happy? ______________________________

____

Thoughts
Child 4

Take Action

We all THINK about things differently

Dulcy and Dion saw their friend Stuart the Seal and they both waved to him. Stuart did not wave back to them. Dulcy and Dion had different thoughts about this situation:

Activity

Answer the questions on the lines below

How would Dulcy's thoughts make her feel? ______________________

What might Dulcy's actions be? ______________________

How would Dion's thoughts make him feel? ______________________

What might Dion's actions be? ______________________

____

____

We can THINK about the same situation in different ways. Scared thoughts make children feel anxious, get Anxious Body Signals and do things that are not helpful (like Dulcy saying she will never talk to Stuart again)

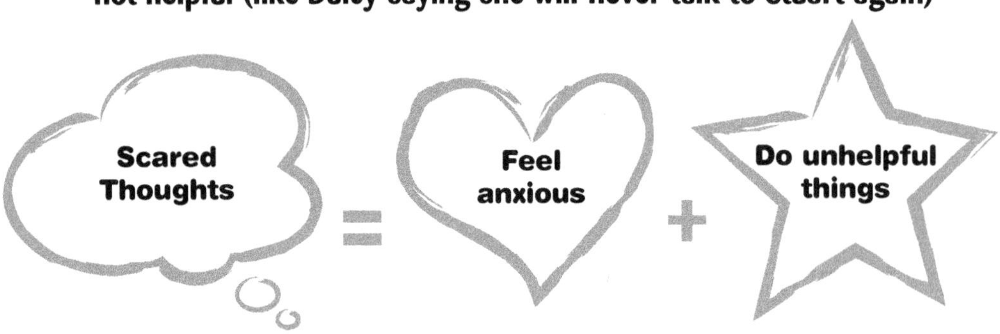

Scared Thoughts

- **Scared Thoughts** make you feel anxious (or Hot on the Feelometer) when you could feel Cool and relaxed.
- **Scared Thoughts** send off 'false alarms' and give you Anxious Body Signals, like a fast beating heart.
- **Scared Thoughts** are unhelpful and make children miss out on fun things because they are too scared to try them.

Catching thoughts by being AWARE of Anxious Body Signals

You can catch Scared Thoughts by being AWARE of your Anxious Body Signals.

Activity

THINK of a time when you felt anxious.

I felt anxious when ______________________________

Rate your Feelings on the Feelometer: ______________________________

What Anxious Body Signals do you remember having? ______________________________

____

____

What made you feel scared in that situation? ______________________________

____

____

What did you think was going to happen in that situation? ______________________________

____

What did you do when you felt anxious in that situation? ______________________________

____

____

Take Action

Thoughts
Child 6

Activity
Catching thoughts by being AWARE

Look at this picture and write down your answers below to practise being AWARE of your thoughts:

Rate your Feelings on the Feelometer: ______________________

What Anxious Body Signals do you notice having? ______________________

____

What thoughts come to mind? ______________________

____

What do you think would happen in this situation? ______________________

____

Write down any other thoughts you noticed having:

____

____

____

Take Action

Activity

Catching thoughts by rewinding your mind!

THINK about your favourite sportsperson or celebrity.

Write down the person's name:

____

Now THINK about this person in great detail. THINK about what they look like, what they do, and what their best performance has been.

Pretend your mind is like a DVD — rewind it back to when you first started thinking about your favourite person and remember what you were thinking. This is what you can do to catch thoughts when you are AWARE that you feel anxious. You can ask yourself "what was I just thinking about?" and then "play back" the situation in your mind to catch your thoughts. Tell the person next to you everything that you thought of about this sportsperson or celebrity.

Once you have caught your Scared Thoughts, you can swap them with Strong and Helpful Thoughts!

Take Action

Thoughts
Child 8

Strong Thoughts

- **Strong Thoughts** help you when you feel anxious.
- **Strong Thoughts** make you feel Cool and relaxed, instead of Hot on the Feelometer.
- **Strong Thoughts** help you to find out that the things you fear are not so scary, that they can be fun, and you can cope!

Strong Thoughts make you feel Strong, they are like big muscles that can help you take ACTION against anxiety!

Activity
Finding Strong Thoughts: How Likely Is That?

My teacher is frowning. You think "He is angry at me".
But ask yourself "How likely is that?"

Thoughts	*He is angry at me*	*He has his mind on something else*	*He is not actually frowning at me*
Clues this is true	*He is frowning*	*He was just talking on the phone before*	*He is looking at the other children being noisy*
Clues this is false	*He is not looking at me.* *I have done all my work*	*He is looking at the other children being noisy*	*He smiled at me a few minutes ago*
Tick the most likely	✗	✗	✔

Take Action

Thoughts
Child 10

Activity

Finding Your Strong Thoughts: How Likely Is That?

Think of a scary time and write your Scared Thought in one piece of the pie graph below. Ask yourself "HOW LIKELY IS THAT?" Then think of two other thoughts and fill in the table below to work out the most likely thought.

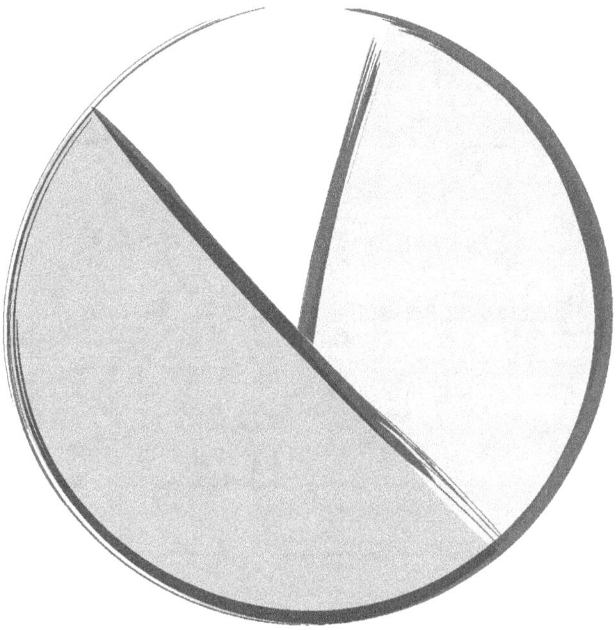

Thoughts			
Clues this is true			
Clues this is false			
Tick the most likely			

Thoughts
Child 11

Take Action

Activity

Finding Strong Thoughts: I Can Cope!

Sometimes situations can be a bit scary or uncomfortable (like going to the doctor or dentist). At these times, Strong Thoughts need to focus on coping ("I can do it"; "keep CALM")! What might be a scary time for you?

____

____

My ACTION plan

I will Keep CALM by:

____

____

____

My Strong Thoughts are:

____

____

____

Activity

Finding Strong Thoughts: Think of all the Options

Some children find speaking in front of the class really scary. They worry that other kids will laugh at them. When you feel anxious about a situation, you might THINK that the Scared Thought is true.

BUT there is always more than one Option in any situation.

Can you THINK of any other things that could happen if you had to speak in front of the class? Write all the possible options (both Scared and Strong Thoughts) you can THINK of in the thought bubbles below. Circle whether each option you have written down is a Scared or Strong Thought.

What is the best option to THINK in this situation? ________________________

Remember: Scared Thoughts are only thoughts! You can find a Strong Thought in every situation. A Strong Thought is always the best option!

Take Action

Keeping Strong Thoughts: Strength Sayings

It is helpful to use catchy Strength Sayings to remember Strong Thoughts. Circle Strength Sayings below that might help you to keep focusing on Strong Thoughts.

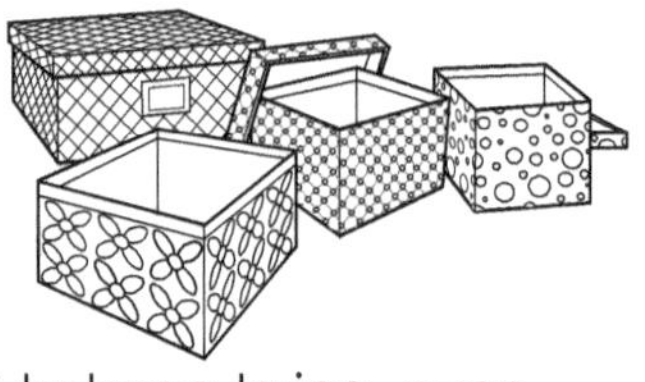

(1) "How likely is that?" or (2) "What's the chances?"
These Strength Sayings help you to look for clues of how likely a Scared thought is and to find other options.

(3) "One step at a time" or (4) "Keep CALM" or (5) "I can do it"
These Strength Sayings remind you that you can cope and to keep trying, even if it feels hard.

(6) "Thoughts are just thoughts"
Our brains are like clever computers — they can think up all sorts of things. Saying to yourself "thoughts are just thoughts" reminds you not to be frightened or worried about thoughts. After all, a "thought is just a thought!"

(7) "In one ear and out the other"
This Strength Saying reminds you that you don't have to focus on every thought you have. You can imagine the thought going in one ear and floating out the other side!

(8) "Keep or Sweep?" or (9) "Throw it away!"
These Strength Sayings remind you that you can decide to keep Strong thoughts and discard Scary thoughts.

(10) "Keep your mind where your body is!"
Sometimes your mind can race ahead and you might worry about things in the future. This can make it hard to concentrate on what you are doing at the time. Saying to yourself 'keep your mind where your body is" can help bring your thoughts back to what you are doing.

(11) "Let it go!"
You could use this Strength Saying when you catch a Scary Thought or find yourself thinking about something over and over, like when you might be worrying about something.

(12) "Bring it on!"
You might use this Strength Saying when you have to do something that's a bit hard or uncomfortable but you have to do it (e.g., get a vaccination). This Strength Saying reminds you to take Action.

(13) "Do the opposite!"
You might catch a Scared Thought that tells you to avoid something. You could say to yourself "Do the opposite" and you might find out the situation wasn't as bad as you thought, and that you could handle it.

Keeping Strong Thoughts: Strength Cards

Dion has just realised that he has been worrying about being late for his swimming class. He noticed he had some Anxious Body Signals, like a fast beating heart and he felt sick in his stomach. Once he noticed these Anxious Body Signals, he was able to catch his Scared Thought. Dion thought about all his OPTIONS in this situation and came up with a Strong Thought (see below)

Dion did a great job in finding a Strong Thought to weaken his Scared Thought. His Anxious Body Signals went away after thinking the Strong Thought and doing On the Spot Deep Breathing. Dion is going to make a Strength Card to strengthen his Strong Thoughts more.

Strength Cards

Strength Cards can help remind you of Strong Thoughts. On one side of a Strength Card, you write the Scared Thought that you are trying to weaken. On the other side of the Strength Card, you write the Strong Thought that you want to keep thinking.

SIDE 1 **Scared Thought**	SIDE 2 **Strong Thought**
I will be late and it will be so bad – I'll get into trouble.	I have everything ready. I will be on time.

Dion is going to keep his Strength Card with him during the day so that he can keep reminding himself of his Strong Thought

This page is intentionally blank.

Take Action

Into Action
Child 1

Step Four

I can Get INTO ACTION by climbing the steps of my ACTION Ladder and rewarding myself.

Dulcy started Grade 4 this year but she is having lots of trouble going to school. She is really afraid of swimming to school by herself. Her home is only 30 metres from her school but she can't go to school without her mum swimming with her. Dulcy wants to be able to swim to school by herself, like the other sea animals can — this is one of her Take ACTION Goals.

Dulcy has created an ACTION Ladder for swimming to school (see below). She has broken down her goal of swimming to school by herself into four smaller steps. These make up the steps in her ACTION Ladder and this will help her to take ACTION slowly, one step at a time. The first step is the smallest and easiest — it must be something that she knows she can do. Each step gets bigger but she will only move onto the next step when she feels CALM and relaxed (Cool on the Feelometer). Dulcy has to remember to use the skills in the ACTION plan — be AWARE of her Anxious Feelings and Body Signals, keep CALM by doing her Breathing and Relaxation and THINK Strong Thoughts — while she climbs the ACTION Ladder.

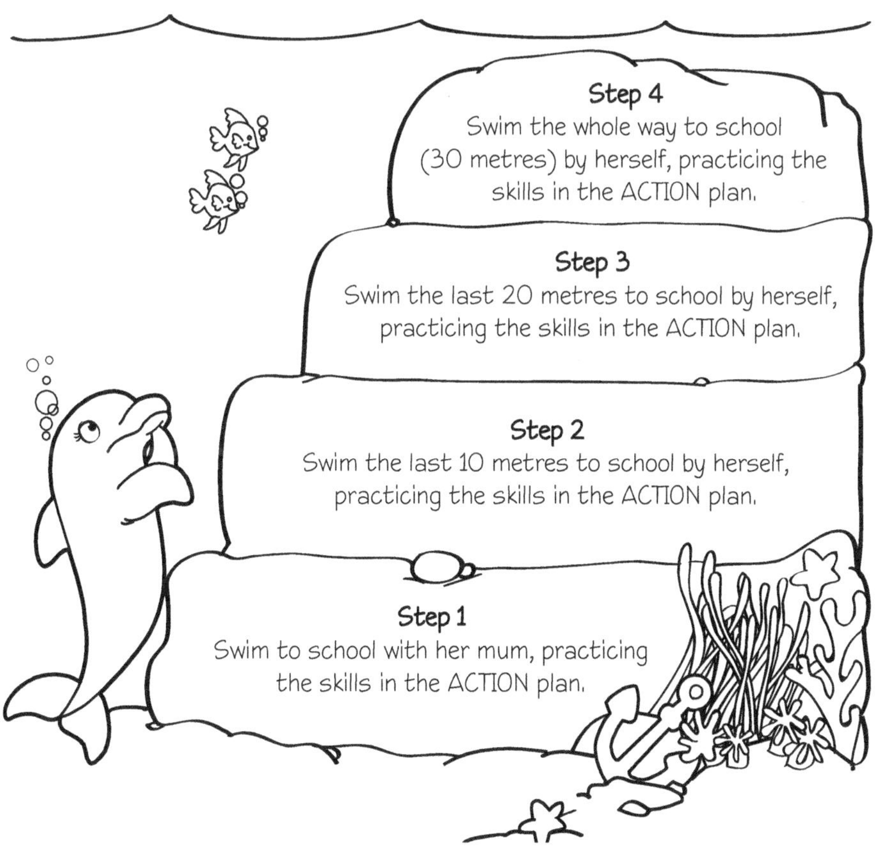

Into Action
Child 2

Take Action

Activity
Practise Makes Perfect

Practise identifying steps you could work towards for one of your Take ACTION goals. You can add more steps to the top if you need to.

Activity
My First Take ACTION Ladder

My Take ACTION Goal: ____

Write each smaller Goal and your Reward (★) in each Step below, starting at Step 1 which is the easiest and then working up the Steps.

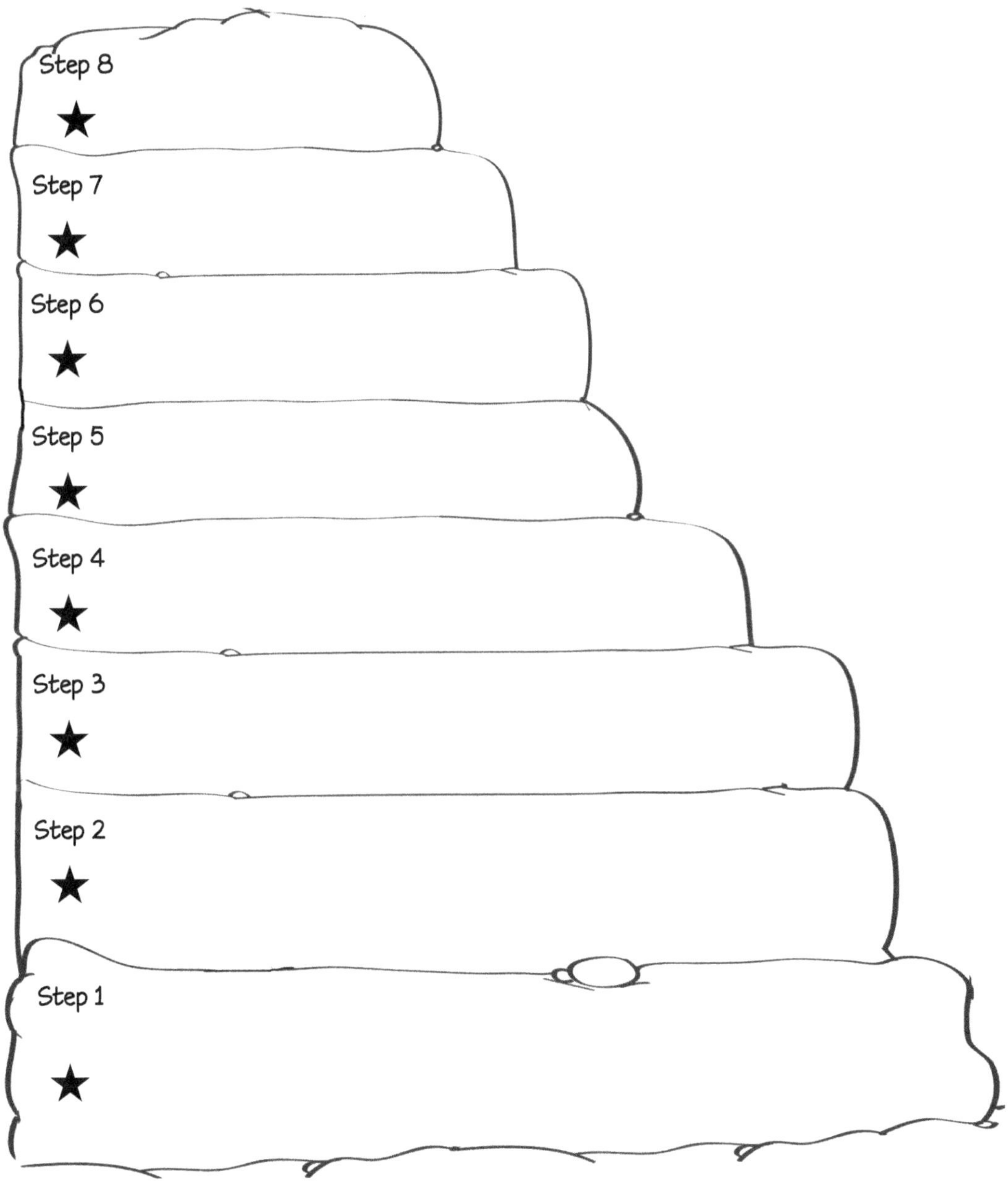

Into Action
Child 4

Take Action

Activity

Small steps towards my First ACTION Ladder

My Take ACTION Goal for My Ladder ______________________________

____

Step on the ACTION Ladder	Fear (0-8)	Rank the steps

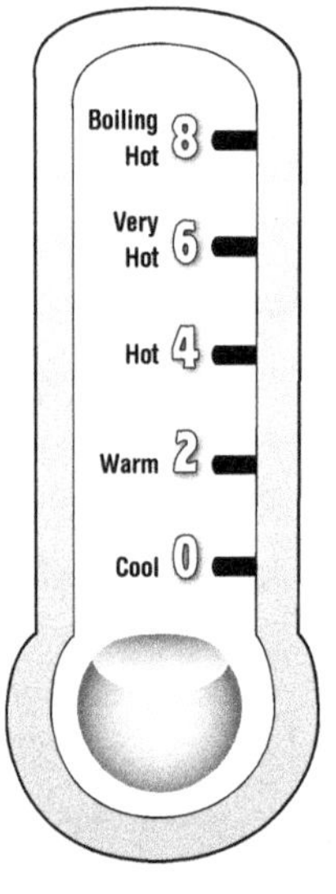

Take Action

Activity
Small rewards towards my First ACTION Ladder

THINK of how you could reward yourself for climbing the steps on your ACTION Ladder. Remember rewards are not only money or other material things. Rewards can be things that you like to do (e.g., special outings) or things that make you feel good (e.g., playing on the computer) or even telling yourself you've done a good job. Write some possible rewards in the stars below:

Reward:

Reward:

Reward:

Reward:

Reward:

Reward:

This page is intentionally blank.

Take Action

Options
Child 1

Step Five

I can use my OPTIONS including Problem Solving, Strong Team, and to Focus on the Positives.

The first OPTION is Problem Solving

Dion wants to go to his friend's birthday party but he is worried no one will talk to him. One way he can solve this problem is to think of other OPTIONS and look at the ACTION he would take for each one to decide what is the best solution.

1. Thought OPTIONS List two thoughts you could have about this scary time.	**2. What type of thought is this (Scared; Strong)?**	**3. What ACTION would you take if you thought this way?**
Option One No one will talk to me. I'll look like I've got no friends.	**Scared Thought** →	• Feel nervous • Feel left out • Not talk to anyone • Miss out on fun things • Leave early
Option Two I feel nervous but it might be good fun.	**Strong Thought** →	• Talk about it with my parents • Arrive with a friend • Use Breathing and Strong Thoughts • Try to join in • Stay for 1 hour, then longer the next time.

4. Weigh up the OPTIONS — What is the best Option for Dion to choose (Look at the ACTION column to decide)? ______________________________

____

5. Take ACTION — Dion does what he has listed in the ACTION column of the Strong Thought Option.

Activity
Problem Solving Practice

THINK about a scary time that you have had recently. Write the scary time in Option One below. Find another solution by thinking of a Strong OPTION and then weighing up the ACTION you would take for each one. Which is best?

1. Thought OPTIONS List two thoughts you could have about this scary time.	**2. What type of thought is this (Scared; Strong)?**	**3. What ACTION would you take if you thought this way?**
Option One		
Option Two		

4. Weigh up the OPTIONS — What is the best Option to choose (Look at the ACTION column to decide)? ____

____

5. Take ACTION — Do what you have listed in the ACTION column of the Strong Thought Option

Take Action

Options
Child 3

The second OPTION is a Strong Team

A Strong Team is a list of people who can help you to feel Strong and take ACTION against your anxiety. Strong Team members are positive people who can remind you of the skills in the ACTION plan.

Activity

Think of people that could be on your Strong Team.

Choose people from home (e.g., parents), school (e.g., teacher) and other areas of your life (e.g., sporting coach) so you can always have a Strong Team member close by. Write your Strong Team members on the lines below.

My Strong Team members are:

1.______________________________

2.______________________________

3.______________________________

4.______________________________

5.______________________________

What situations could your Strong Team members help you with?

____

____

What could your Strong Team members do to help you (e.g., listen to you, remind you of the skills in the ACTION plan)?

____

____

Ask the people you listed above if they will be part of your Strong Team. Tell your Strong Team members what situations they can help you with, and how they can best help you to take ACTION against anxiety.

Options
Child 4

Take Action

The third OPTION is to Focus on the Positives

Remember from the "THINK Strong Thoughts" Module that Strength Sayings are catchy sayings that will help you to feel Strong as you are taking ACTION against anxiety.

Some examples of Strength Sayings are:

I can do it!

I am Strong!

Activity

Now that you have more experience feeling strong by doing your ACTION Ladder, think about some more Strength Sayings that you can use to keep feeling Strong.

Write your Strength Sayings in the ribbons below:

Take Action

Options
Child 5

Keep Being Positive

Here are helpful things you can do to keep Being Positive:

Keep your body active and try new things!

Smile a lot!

Think about nice things you enjoy!

Believe in yourself and never give up!

Keep doing these things so you Feel Strong like Dulcy and Dion.

Activity
Things I can do well

Try to list as many positive things about yourself as possible. These can be things you do well (e.g., I'm a good swimmer) or things you like about yourself (e.g., I'm friendly towards other people). Try to be creative and list EVERYTHING you can think of.

Activity
Things I like about me

Take Action

Options
Child 7

A Story from Dulcy

Dulcy can see that you have learnt three more OPTIONS so far to use when taking ACTION against anxiety. The first Option is Problem Solving, which helps you to find the best Option to deal with a scary time. The second Option is a Strong Team that is full of people who can help remind you of the skills in the ACTION plan. The third Option is to Focus on the Positives. Strength Sayings will help you feel Strong when you are taking ACTION. It is also important to focus on the good things about yourself, other people and the world around you. Remind yourself of the things you do well and what you like about yourself. Dulcy thinks that using all these OPTIONS will help you take ACTION and feel happy.

Activity

Dulcy would like to ask you what you have learnt so far during the Use My OPTIONS step

Write down your answers on the lines below:

____

____

____

____

____

____

The fourth OPTION is having Confident Body Signals

Children who get anxious often find it hard to talk to other people and stand up for themselves, and they might get bullied. Showing Confident Body Signals can help you to be confident, assertive and deal with bullies.

Remember back to when you learnt about Anxious Body Signals (e.g. fast beating heart). You now know how to keep CALM (by using On the Spot Deep Breathing and Move my Muscles Relaxation) to reduce these Anxious Body Signals.

Confident Body Signals help you to look Confident in social situations (e.g. talking with a friend at school). There is an easy way to remember your Strong Confident Body Signals — just remember to:

SMILE

S Smile and face the other person.

M MAKE eye contact and look interested while you are talking with the other person.

I INITIATE the conversation.
Remember to:
- Use a greeting (e.g., "Hello") when introducing yourself
- Pick a topic that you both like to talk about
- Ask questions

L LISTEN to the other person.

E ENJOY yourself and relax:
- Use On the Spot Deep Breathing
- Remember your Strength Sayings
- Keep smiling

Take Action

Options
Child 9

Take ACTION Task One

Write down some good conversation topics on the lines below

____

____

____

____

Pick a topic to talk about with your partner. Practise using your Confident Body Signals (SMILE) while you talk about this topic.

How did you feel on the Feelometer before the Take ACTION Task?

____

How did you feel on the Feelometer after the Take ACTION Task?

____

How did your Confident Body Signals help you during the Take ACTION Task?

____

____

Start practising SMILE with your family and friends. Using Confident Body Signals will help you to look Confident and keep taking ACTION against anxiety!

The fifth OPTION is Being Confident and Assertive

Look at the three different ways that you can act towards other children and adults below.

The Shy Starfish Way

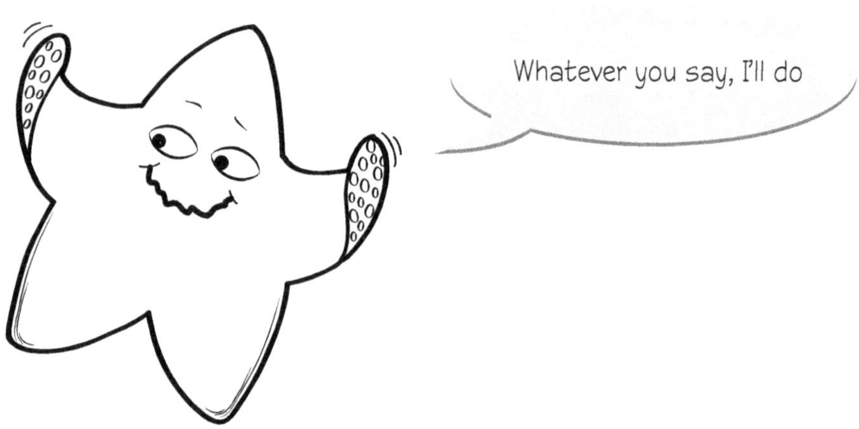

Acting like the Shy Starfish means you might ignore the situation or 'give in' to the other person. You do not say how you feel about the situation.

- **Feelings:** Shy, embarrassed, nervous, useless, unhappy.
- **Body Signals:** Talk softly like a mouse, mumble, look down at the floor, stand far away, hunch over, feel Hot on the Feelometer.
- **You might say things like:** "Whatever you say", "I don't know", "If you say so".
- **Actions:** You might do things like walk away, not be able to say NO, give the other person what they want (even if you don't want to!), avoid the problem, get upset.

Do you think that this is a good way to act?

☐ YES ☐ NO

Take Action

Options
Child 10B

The Angry Shark Way

Acting like the Angry Shark means you attack the other person, over-react or get angry at the other person.

- **Feelings:** Angry, annoyed, out of control, mean.
- **Body signals:** Stand close to the other person, look angry, have tight muscles and clenched fists, feel Hot on the Feelometer.
- **You might say things like:** "You'd better do this for me", "If you don't do this, watch out", "I want this now".
- **Actions:** You might do things like look angry, threaten, push, hit, kick, shout, yell, speak rudely or tease.

Do you think that this is a good way to act?

☐ **YES** ☐ **NO**

Options
Child 10C

Take Action

The Strong Dolphin Way: Being Confident and Assertive

Acting like the Strong Dolphin means you say how you feel and speak up for yourself in an honest, polite and friendly way. This is called being Assertive!

- **Feelings:** Happy, confident, in control and you feel good about yourself.
- **Body signals:** Stand tall, smile, look CALM, look others in the eyes, feel Cool on the Feelometer.
- **You might say things like:** "I THINK that...", "Let's try", "I would like to do it this way".
- **Actions:** You might do things like speak firmly but friendly, be confident and relaxed, listen to the other person's point of view, speak up for your rights, find a solution to the problem and make more friends.

Do you think that this is a good way to act?

☐ YES ☐ NO

Three Steps to being Confident and Assertive

Dulcy would like to act in a Confident and Assertive way with her friend but she doesn't know how to. Dulcy's friend borrowed her swimming cap three weeks ago and she hasn't given it back to her. Dulcy really needs her swimming cap so she can keep climbing her ACTION Ladder of swimming to school by herself. Let's help Dulcy to be Confident and Assertive by following the steps below.

Step One: **Tell the other person what you think the problem is**

Sally, when you borrowed my swimming cap three weeks ago, I thought you would give it back to me after your lesson.

Step Two: **Tell the other person how you feel about the problem**

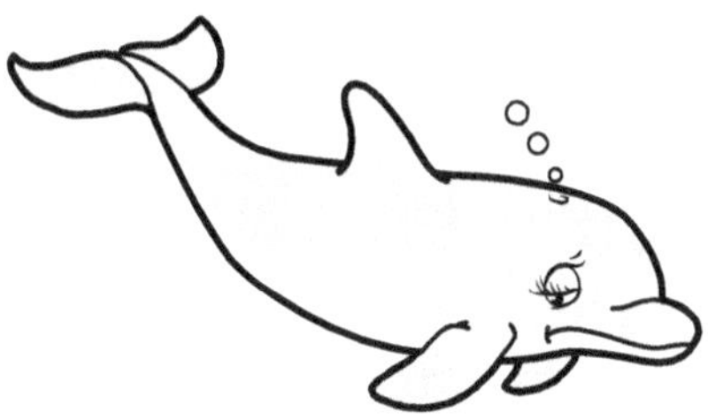

I feel annoyed that you haven't given my swimming cap back.

Step Three: **Tell the other person a solution to the problem**

I would really like it if you gave me my swimming cap back today.

Things to remember when being Confident and Assertive:

- Use your Confident Body Signals (SMILE).
- Keep CALM by doing On the Spot Deep Breathing
- THINK Strong Thoughts.
- Discuss the solution you have thought of with the other person. Remember to listen to their point of view as well!

Congratulate yourself if you tried to be Confident and Assertive!!

Take Action

Take ACTION Task Two

Read the two stories below. Write a Confident and Assertive way of acting following the three steps listed. After you have written down a Confident and Assertive response, role play each situation with a partner.

Story One

Your friend has been bossing you around at lunch time.You have decided you don't want to be bossed around anymore.

Step One: **Tell the other person what you think the problem is**

Step Two: **Tell the other person how you feel about the problem**

Step Three: **Tell the other person a solution to the problem**

Take Action

Options
Child 12B

Story Two

Your friend wants to copy answers from a Maths test you studied hard for.

Step One: Tell the other person what you think the problem is

Step Two: Tell the other person how you feel about the problem

Step Three: Tell the other person a solution to the problem

Options
Child 13

Take Action

The sixth OPTION is learning the Steps for Dealing with Bullying.

There are different ways that children can be bullied. Some examples of bullying include:

- Being made fun of for something you said or did;
- Other kids saying mean things about you to others or to you;
- Someone teasing you about your looks or because you are different from them;
- Being left out of activities;
- Being physically hurt or your property damaged.

Why do children bully others?

- They think they are cool or powerful, but bullies are usually not confident themselves. They bully others to make themselves feel good.
- They might be jealous of something good about you.
- They are bored.
- They are trying to "push your buttons" and get a reaction – they want to be noticed or get attention.

If you react to the bullying, the bully gets what they want: a reaction.

It is helpful to deal with bullying by being Confident and Assertive (like you have learnt already) and following the steps for Dealing with Bullying.

Steps for Dealing with Bullying

Step One: Stop what you are doing and practise your On the Spot Deep Breathing. This will help you to keep CALM.

Step Two: THINK about the OPTIONS that you have in the situation. Some Strong and Confident OPTIONS to choose from are:

Walk away

Tell an adult

Ignore the bullying if you can

Say "I heard what you said and I don't really care"

Tell them firmly and calmly to leave you alone

Imagine there is a force field all around you protecting you from their words

Step Three: Decide on the best Option and take ACTION. Say how you feel in a Confident and Assertive way (like the Strong Dolphin).

Things to remember when Dealing with Bullying:

- Use your Confident Body Signals (SMILE).
- Keep CALM by doing On the Spot Deep Breathing.
- THINK Strong Thoughts.
- Do not yell or scream, call them names, or be physically aggressive.

Congratulate yourself for dealing with this situation!

Options
Child 15

Take Action

Activity

Dion has been bullied by Shawn the Shark at school for the last few weeks. Shawn says things to Dion like:

Write down what Dion should do at each step for dealing with Shawn's bullying:

Step One: ____________________

Step Two: Circle which Strong and Confident OPTIONS Dion should choose.

- Walk away
- Tell an adult
- Ignore the bullying if you can
- Say "I heard what you said and I don't really care"
- Tell them firmly and calmly to leave you alone
- Imagine there is a force field all around you protecting you from their words

What is the best Option for Dion to choose? ____________________

Take Action

Take ACTION Task Three

Role play the situation that you have just helped Dion with. Remember to follow the three Steps for Dealing with Bullying with your partner.

Do you think you could use these steps yourself if you are bullied in the future? Circle one of the boxes below.

Yes! I could use these steps!	Yes! But I think I need a bit more practice!

If the bullying keeps going talk to your parents, and your teacher if it happened at school. You could also talk to your Strong Team members to work out a plan of ACTION.

Story from Dulcy

Dulcy can see that you have learnt three more OPTIONS to use in your ACTION Plan. Using Confident Body Signals (SMILE); being Confident and Assertive (like the Strong Dolphin) with other children and adults; and learning the Steps for Dealing with Bullying will help you to keep taking ACTION against situations that worry you. Dulcy thinks that if you keep taking ACTION against anxiety, you will learn that you are a Strong and Confident person. You will be able to enjoy things more and be happy. Keep up the great work!

Activity

Dulcy would like to ask you what you have learnt during the Use My OPTIONS step.

"Write down your answers on the lines below.

____

____

This page is intentionally blank.

Take Action

Never Stop
Child 1

N Step Six

I will NEVER stop taking ACTION against anxiety

You have done a great job learning to Take ACTION against anxiety

You have learnt six steps in the ACTION plan to help you deal with anxiety. It is important that you NEVER stop taking ACTION in the future.

By planning for times in the future when you may need your ACTION plan, you will already be prepared and Strong!

Activity

For each of the six steps in the ACTION plan, write down the skills that will help you take ACTION against anxiety in the future.

A **Be AWARE** ____

C **Keep CALM** ____

T **THINK Strong Thoughts** ____

I **Get INTO Action** ____

O **Use my OPTIONS** ____

N **NEVER stop taking ACTION** ____

Never Stop
Child 2A

Take Action

Let's put the steps into ACTION — Jack's Story

Jack feels anxious about going to school. Here's how he took ACTION to overcome his fears.

A

Be AWARE

When I wake up in the morning, I am AWARE that I am feeling anxious. I have Anxious Body Signals like butterflies in my stomach and a fast beating heart. I would rate myself as Boiling Hot on the Feelometer.

C

Keep CALM

I use my Move my Muscles Relaxation while I am lying in bed to get calmer. I feel much better after I tense and relax my face, shoulders, hands, stomach, legs and feet. While I am getting ready for school, I use my On the Spot Deep Breathing. When I slowly breathe in and out, I feel more relaxed. I can also use my Breathing at school if I start to feel anxious.

T

THINK Strong Thoughts

I THINK Strong Thoughts, like "I don't need to be anxious, I have my favourite lesson today". I will take the Strength Card that I made for this scary time and keep it in my shorts pocket — that way I can look at it if I feel anxious. Thinking Strong Thoughts helps me to feel Strong and Confident.

I

Get INTO Action

I Get INTO Action to learn to feel calm going to school by using an ACTION Ladder (see over page). The steps on my ACTION ladder get bigger but I can take it slowly — one step at a time. I reward myself for taking ACTION on each step of the Ladder.

O

Use my OPTIONS

I have other OPTIONS to use when I feel anxious as well. I could say my favourite Strength Saying "I can do this" to myself. My mum reminds me to take ACTION — she is part of my Strong Team. I also use Problem Solving at school if I need to. I Keep Focusing on the Positives and be confident with other children by using SMILE and Being Assertive!

N

NEVER stop taking ACTION

I will NEVER stop taking ACTION against feeling anxious when I go to school. I know that sometimes it will be hard and sometimes it will be easy.
I can use all the skills in my Action Plan to Be AWARE, to Keep CALM, to THINK Strong Thoughts, to Get INTO Action and use all my OPTIONS. I know that I will enjoy school more and be happier if I keep taking ACTION.

Jack's ACTION Ladder

I have to stay on each step of my ACTION Ladder until I feel CALM and relaxed (Cool on the Feelometer). If I have difficulty with any of the steps on my ACTION Ladder, I need to practise that step until I master it.

You can make a story for your own scary times.
Remember to use all the steps in the ACTION plan when writing your story!

Never Stop
Child 3

Take Action

Activity

Think back to when you first started the Take Action program and you were not feeling as Strong or Confident about facing anxiety.

Draw a picture or write some words in the box below that shows how you felt before you knew the steps in the ACTION plan.

Take Action

Never Stop
Child 4

Activity

Now think about how you feel after completing the Take Action program. Think about the Take Action Goals that you have achieved.

Draw a picture or write some words in the box below that shows how Strong and Confident you feel because you now have an ACTION plan.

Things my therapist noticed about my progress during the Take Action Program.

Activity

Looking Ahead — NEVER Stop Taking ACTION

Think about scary times you still have now, or times in the future that you might find scary. An example of a future scary time might be starting a new grade at school. Knowing what some of these scary times might be means you can use your ACTION Plan when you need it! Write down some future scary times on the lines below.

Scary times might be: ______________________________

____

Activity

For each of the six steps in the ACTION plan, write down the skills that will help you take ACTION against anxiety in the future.

A ______________________________

C ______________________________

T ______________________________

I ______________________________

O ______________________________

N ______________________________

My ACTION Ladder

Talk with your parents about the scary times you have written down previously. Choose one of these scary times and create another ACTION Ladder.

My Take ACTION Goal ____

____

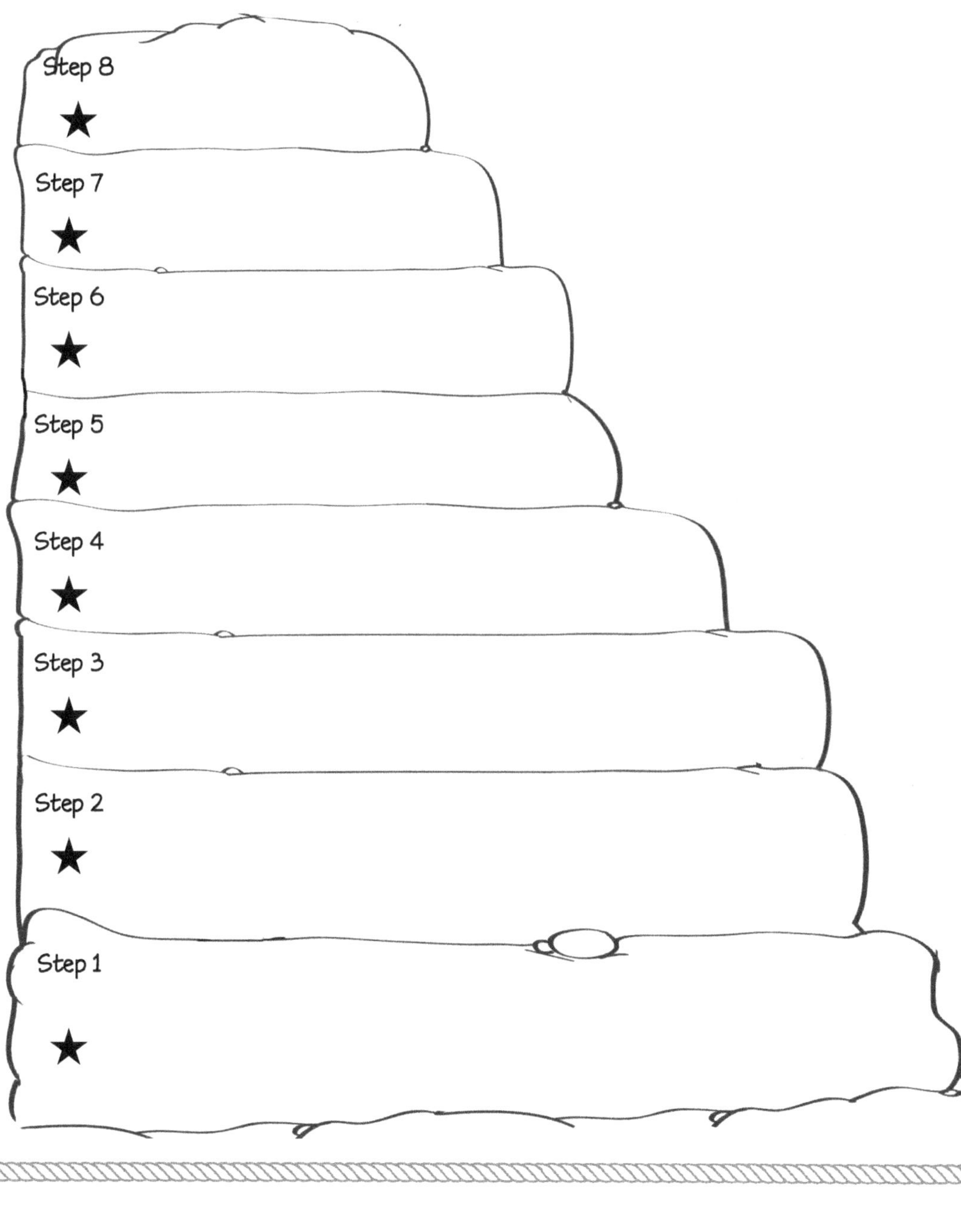

A Story from Dulcy and Dion!

Dulcy and Dion can see you have learnt about how to keep taking ACTION in the future. Dulcy and Dion know that they have learnt a lot from the Take Action program and they hope you have too! Dulcy and Dion think you should put your Take ACTION bookmark and this workbook somewhere safe so that you can read about your ACTION plan whenever you need to. Dulcy and Dion have really enjoyed doing the Take Action program with you. Remember to NEVER stop taking ACTION in the future and your anxiety will stay away. Dulcy and Dion wish you all the best for the future and hope that you continue to be strong and happy!

Activity

Dulcy and Dion would like to ask you what you have learnt in the NEVER stop taking Action step. On the lines below, write down your answer.

During the NEVER stop taking Action step, I learnt

____

____

____

Always remember: You can feel better about anything that scares or worries you by using your

ACTION

Plan!

Take Action

Congratulations
to

....

on completing
The
Take Action
Program!

You now have an ACTION Plan to use in the future whenever you need to take ACTION against anxiety!

.... Practitioner's Signature

.... Date

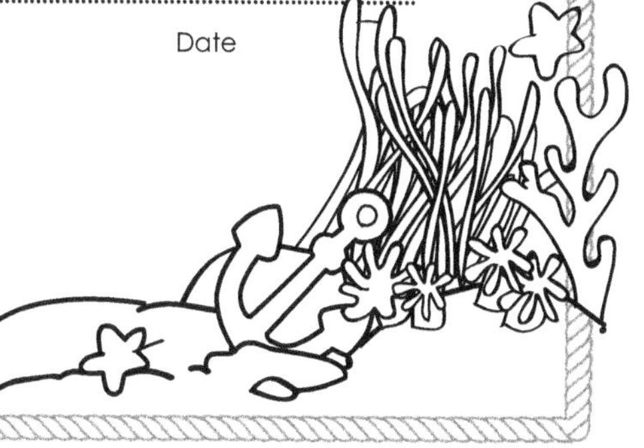

Appendix B
Parent Handouts

Module 1

A — Be Aware

Module 2

C — Keep Calm

Module 3

T — Strong Thoughts

Module 4

I — Into Action

Module 5

O — Options

Module 6

N — Never Stop

A Be AWARE

WELCOME to the Take Action program

The first step in the ACTION plan teaches children to be AWARE of their feelings and recognise when they feel anxious. Children will also learn to be AWARE of signals in their bodies that indicate they are feeling anxious.

Parenting can be a rewarding **and** challenging experience.

When a child experiences anxiety to the point where they miss out on enjoying some things in life, parents are presented with many challenges.

Often parents want to help their child but are not sure what to do, or they have already tried numerous things in the past.

The Take Action program has been designed to assist children and their families in managing anxiety.

Children (and their parents) will learn how to cope with and manage anxiety by Taking

ACTION

Taking ACTION against anxiety can help children enjoy life and be happy!

Children will create a Strong Team — a supportive network of people that can help them to take ACTION against their anxiety. It would be great if parents can start being part of their child's Strong Team straight away. This means that you will help your child practise the new skills they will learn, and provide support and encouragement to them as they progress through the Take Action program.

It is important to check with your child and see what they are learning and what Home Tasks they have to complete each week. The skills learnt in the Take Action program need to become a part of your child's daily life if they are to reduce their anxiety.

Be Aware
Parent 2

Take Action

Structure of the Take Action program

Parents are a very important part of the Take Action program. Parents will be introduced to the principles of the program, in addition to learning helpful parenting strategies that will assist them in encouraging their child to take ACTION against anxiety.

Step in the ACTION Plan	Child Content	Parent Content
	Introduction to the Take Action program	Introduction to the Take Action program
A Be AWARE	Learning to recognise signs of anxiety	Instruction about the Be AWARE and Keep CALM steps
C Keep CALM	Learning relaxation techniques	—
T THINK Strong Thoughts	Learning to THINK positive, ACTION-oriented thoughts	Instruction about the THINK Strong Thoughts step
I Get INTO Action	Learning to approach anxiety-provoking situations	Instruction about the Get INTO Action step
O Use my OPTIONS	Learning additional coping strategies	Instruction about the Use my OPTIONS and NEVER stop taking ACTION steps
N NEVER stop taking Action	Learning to use all the steps in the ACTION plan to keep taking ACTION against anxiety	Instruction about the NEVER stop taking ACTION steps
Booster	Review of the program	Review of the program

Take Action

Be Aware
Parent 3

What is anxiety in children?

Anxiety is a common emotion that we all experience. Everyone feels scared or worried at some time — it is a normal part of life.

Anxiety is a signal that there is danger. In the caveman days, it was very important for cavemen to get scared if they saw a sabre-tooth tiger so they could either fight the tiger or run away to safety (see below).

It is normal to feel scared when you are in real danger, but sometimes children get scared or worried when they don't need to. Things like making new friends or being in the dark or being away from their parents might seem extremely scary to some children. These "false alarms" are not really dangerous but children might THINK they are. Children can learn that making new friends can be lots of fun and that they can be safe even when it is dark or when they are on their own.

All children experience anxiety as part of normal development. Many fears such as fear of the dark, fear of being away from parents and fear of strangers are normal and common aspects of child development and are thought to help protect children from danger and harm. However, when children experience excessive distress or they find it difficult to do things that other children of their age are capable of doing (because of their worries or fears), anxiety can be considered a problem.

Anxiety is one of the most common problems in children. Estimates differ, but approximately 1 in 10 children experience high levels of anxiety.

Types of anxiety in children

Children (and adults) experience anxiety in different ways. The Take Action program has been designed to target four different types of anxiety in children:

Generalised Anxiety: Children who have a general tendency to be worried about a range of life areas. Children typically worry about future events, past behaviour, academic or athletic achievement, friends, and health. Children often engage in excessive reassurance seeking, are often perfectionistic and highly conscientious. A number of physical complaints are usually reported including sleep disturbance, feeling tired, general feelings of tension (e.g., easily annoyed or grumpy) and an inability to relax.

Separation Anxiety: Children who fear being separated from a main caregiver, usually their mother or father. Children become extremely distressed and frightened whenever they become separated from their caregiver, and may try to avoid things like school or sleeping alone. Children with separation anxiety also worry about the possibility of being kidnapped, and accidents or death occurring, either to themselves or their caregiver. Children often report a number of physical complaints such as headaches, stomach aches or general sickness, especially upon impending separation.

Social Anxiety: Children who fear and/or avoid social situations where they have to interact with other people or be the centre of attention. Children often think others will evaluate them negatively or that they will embarrass themselves.

Specific Fears: Children who have excessive fear of a specific object, activity or situation and avoid this object, activity or situation. Some of the common types of specific phobias in children are fears of animals, natural environment (e.g., darkness, storms, water), blood and / or injections, and situations like elevators.

What causes anxiety in children?

There is no one factor that causes anxiety in children. Anxiety is due to a mix of factors which is likely to be different for every child. Some of these factors include:

Traumatic Event

A child who experiences a traumatic event (e.g., is severely bullied at school) may develop intense fear of this event (e.g., school and / or bullies).

Child Factors

- Temperament of the child — children can be born with an anxious temperament (e.g., shy, reactive, emotional vs. laid back).
- Biology / Genetics — anxiety seems to run in families. Children may have a highly-reactive nervous system (e.g., they are sensitive and quick to react to potential signs of danger).
- Way the child thinks — more likely to 'see' danger in the situation and underestimate his/her ability to cope in the situation (e.g., "What if....").

Learning Factors

↓

Children are influenced by their environment, family, parents, school and peers

- Observation (e.g., seeing a parent frightened by a dog).
- Information they receive (e.g., if a child falls over and a parent shows they are extremely distressed by this, the child may learn that falling over is a terrible thing that should be avoided at all costs).
- Accidental rewards (e.g., a hug is given when they are anxious).
- Avoidance of anxiety-provoking situation — this maintains the child's anxiety about the situation / object.

Activity

Think about the factors that might be important for your child's anxiety. Place an X in the box next to each relevant factor and think about why this factor may be important for your child.

☐ Traumatic events (describe)

____

☐ Temperament (describe)

____

☐ Biology / Genetics (describe)

____

☐ Way your child thinks (describe)

____

☐ Observation (describe)

____

☐ Information your child receives (describe)

____

☐ Accidental rewards (describe)

____

☐ Avoidance (describe)

____

Take Action

Be Aware
Parent 7

Cycle of Anxiety in children

The figure below shows the three response systems of anxiety in children.

Situation / Trigger
Having to present a talk in front of the class

1. Cognitive responses
Children think negatively and attend to threat cues in the situation when they feel anxious.

Example — *Thoughts such as "Everyone will laugh at me" and "I can't do it."*

2. Physiological responses
Children experience a number of body sensations when they feel anxious.

Example — *A child may complain of their heart beating fast or butterflies in their tummy.*

3. Behavioural responses
Children may want to avoid or escape the situation/trigger or show high levels of distress.

Example — *A child may complain of feeling sick because they don't want to go to school on the day of their speech.*

Be Aware
Parent 8

Take Action

How can the Take Action program assist children and families?

The Take Action program aims to teach children helpful ways to cope with and manage anxiety by addressing the Three Responses of Anxiety. The word ACTION is a coping-oriented acronym used throughout the program. Children are encouraged to *Take ACTION* against their anxiety (e.g., approach their fears/worries) using the well-researched and effective strategies learnt during the program.

Children will learn about an ACTION plan, with each letter in the word ACTION standing for a set of skills that children will learn during the program (described below):

Steps in the ACTION Plan

A

Be AWARE — The first step in the ACTION plan teaches children to be AWARE of their feelings and learn to recognise when they feel anxious. Children will also learn to be AWARE of signals in their bodies that indicate they are feeling anxious.

C

Keep CALM — Once children learn to be AWARE of signs of anxiety, the second step in the ACTION plan teaches children strategies to keep CALM and reduce their anxiety. These strategies include On The Spot Deep Breathing and Move My Muscles Relaxation.

T

THINK Strong Thoughts — Building on from being AWARE and keeping CALM, the third step in the ACTION plan teaches children to THINK positively and confidently. Children learn strategies for turning Scared (unhelpful) thoughts into Strong (positive) thoughts.

I

Get INTO ACTION — The fourth step in the ACTION plan encourages children to gradually deal with anxiety-provoking situations using an ACTION Ladder (a step-by-step graded exposure hierarchy). Children practise the Be AWARE, Keep CALM and THINK Strong Thoughts steps while climbing their ACTION Ladder/s. Children are encouraged to reward themselves for taking ACTION against their anxiety.

O

Use my OPTIONS — The fifth step in the ACTION plan teaches children additional strategies (or OPTIONS) to further manage their anxiety including problem solving, asking supportive others for help, and positive self-statements. Children are also taught social skills (e.g., confident body signals, assertiveness, dealing with bullying strategies) to further enhance their coping abilities.

N

NEVER stop taking ACTION — The last step in the ACTION plan encourages children to plan for anxiety-provoking times so they can keep taking ACTION against anxiety in the future.

How the ACTION plan works

Situation / Trigger
Having to present a talk in front of the class

3. Behavioural responses
Children may want to avoid or escape the situation/trigger or show high levels of distress.

Example — *A child may complain of feeling sick because they don't want to go to school on the day of their speech.*

1. Cognitive responses
Children think negatively and attend to threat cues in the situation when they feel anxious.

Example — Thoughts such as "Everyone will laugh at me" and "I can't do it."

2. Physiological responses
Children experience a number of body sensations when they feel anxious.

Example — *A child may complain of their heart beating fast or butterflies in their tummy.*

Relevant skills in the ACTION plan

- **Get INTO Action** — Gradual exposure (Action Ladders) to anxiety-provoking situations, accompanied by self-reward.
- **Use my OPTIONS** — Additional strategies to further manage anxiety, including Problem Solving, and Social Skills.

Relevant skills in the ACTION plan

- **Be AWARE** of Anxious Feelings and Body Signals.
- **Keep CALM** — On the Spot Breathing and Move My Muscle Relaxation to reduce Anxious Feelings and Body Signals.

Relevant skills in the ACTION plan

- **THINK Strong Thoughts** — Replace negative/threat-based thoughts with helpful Strong Thoughts.
- **NEVER stop taking ACTION** — Relapse prevention and maintenance.

Take Action

Personal Goals

In the Take Action program, your child will learn to reduce their anxiety.

Activity

Think about the goals that you have for your child (e.g., I want him/her to be able to sleep in his bed without the light on).

Write your Take ACTION Goals for your child on the lines below:

____

____

____

____

Think about the goals you have for yourself (e.g., I want to learn how to help my child to keep calm when he/she goes to school).

Write your own Take ACTION Goals on the lines below:

____

____

____

____

We will review these goals during the program. Share these goals with your child so they know everyone on their Strong Team will be working together.

Be AWARE: Anxiety is a Good Alarm and a False Alarm

As discussed earlier, it was very important for the caveman to feel scared if he saw a sabre-tooth tiger. As soon as the caveman saw the sabre-tooth tiger, the caveman's brain would send messages of danger to his body, making his heart beat fast and his hands cold. These changes in his body would help him to take ACTION and survive because he could either fight the tiger if he had to, or run away from the tiger to safety.

Children and adults get the same changes in their bodies today. If we have to fight or escape from a dangerous situation, our bodies change to help us to be Strong and take ACTION. This is when anxiety is helpful to us! It is normal to feel scared when you are in real danger — just like the caveman.

A certain amount of anxiety in performance situations, such as sporting events, can also be useful (see figure below). However, if anxiety levels become too high it can stop children from doing things properly and they often avoid situations altogether.

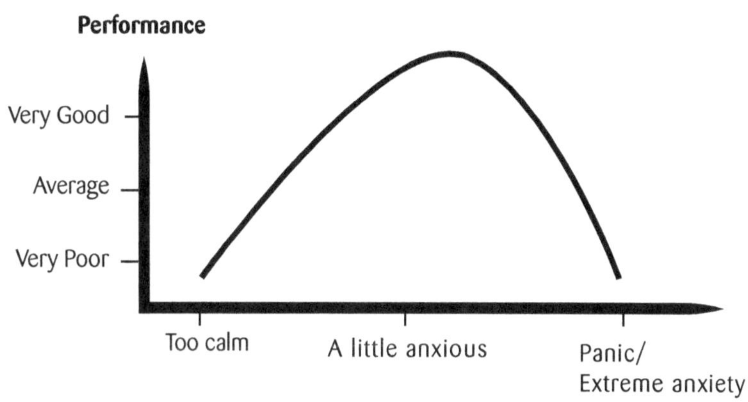

Sometimes children have 'false alarms' and they feel scared in their bodies when there is no real danger. Children only THINK there is danger. When there is a 'false alarm', children feel Hot on the Feelometer when they should feel Cool (this is happening to the boy below). Help your child to be AWARE of these 'false alarms', by encouraging them to work out how anxious they feel on the Feelometer.

False ALARM

Be AWARE of Anxious Feelings

Feelometer

A great way for children to work out how anxious they are feeling in different situations is to use the Feelometer.

Look at the **Feelometer** below:

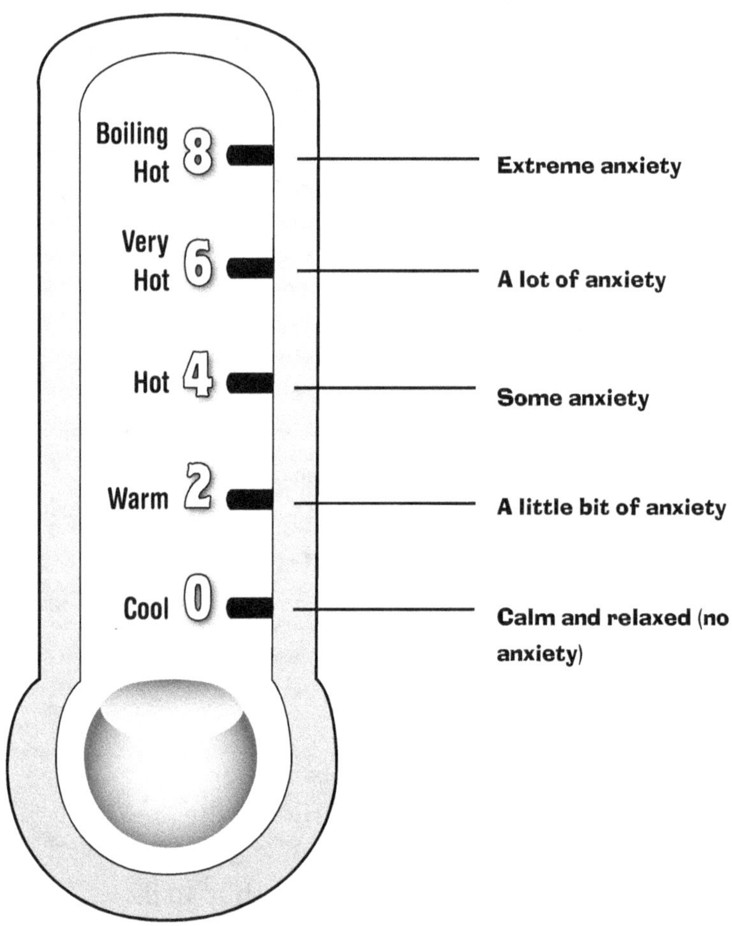

Take Action

Be Aware
Parent 13

Activity
Feelometer

Your child is learning to use the Feelometer to be aware of their anxious feelings. The Feelometer is also a useful tool for parents to help their child identify anxious feelings in different situations. Think about your child's anxiety levels in relation to ratings on the Feelometer.

Write down a time when your child is CALM and relaxed (Cool on the Feelometer):

____

____

Write down a time when your child feels A little bit of anxiety (Warm on the Feelometer):

____

____

Write down a time when your child feels Some anxiety (Hot on the Feelometer):

____

____

Write down a time when your child feels A lot of anxiety (Very Hot on the Feelometer):

____

____

Write down a time when your child feels Extreme anxiety (Boiling Hot on the Feelometer):

____

____

ACTION Parents Can Take

As a parent, you can help your child learn to be aware of their anxious feelings by prompting them to rate how they are feeling on the Feelometer. Once AWARE that they are feeling anxious, your child will be able to take ACTION.

Activity

Be AWARE of Anxious Body Signals

Your child is learning to work out which Anxious Body Signals they get when they feel anxious.

Colour-in the Anxious Body Signals that you have noticed or your child has talked about when they feel anxious. Add in any other Anxious Body Signals that are not listed.

Add in any other Anxious Body Signals that are not listed.

ACTION Parents Can Take

Helping your child to be AWARE of their Anxious Body Signals is very important. Once they are AWARE of their Anxious Body Signals, they will be able to keep CALM and relaxed — this is the second step in the ACTION plan!

Activity
Be AWARE of Anxious Feelings

Faces are another way children can be aware of feelings. Look at the faces below and write down the correct feeling. Think about how your child would show each feeling.

What feeling/s is this face showing?

____

How often does your child feel this way?

____

What feeling/s is this face showing?

____

How often does your child feel this way?

____

What feeling/s is this face showing?

____

How often does your child feel this way?

____

What feeling/s is this face showing?

____

How often does your child feel this way?

____

ACTION Parents Can Take

As a parent, you can help your child to know how he or she is feeling so they can take ACTION to go from Hot to Cool on the Feelometer and stop 'false alarms'. In anxious situations, encourage your child to **Stop**, **Look** for clues in the environment and people's faces, and **Learn** from their body signals so they can take ACTION.

This page is intentionally blank.

Keep CALM

Once children learn to be AWARE of signs of anxiety, the second step in the ACTION plan teaches children strategies to keep CALM.

The first way to keep CALM is to practise On the Spot Deep Breathing.

Deep Breathing can be used whenever children need it and no one has to know they are doing it. That's why it's called "On the Spot" Deep Breathing. It helps children to stay CALM and not let their Anxious Body Signals bother them.

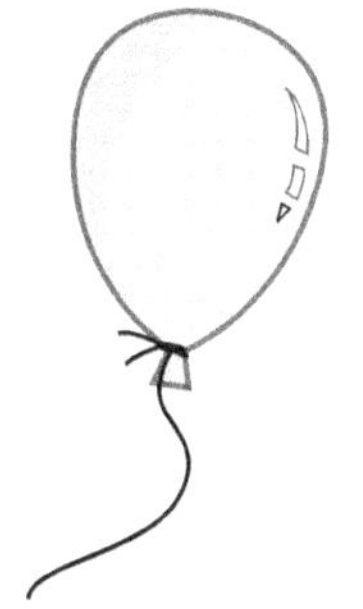

This is how your child is being taught to use Breathing:

1. Place one hand on your stomach and one hand on your chest. Imagine you have a balloon in your stomach and you want to blow it up real big. This means you have to push the air you breathe in all the way down into your stomach.
2. Slowly breathe in through your nose, counting to 3 and "blow up the balloon" in your stomach (make it big like the balloon above). Your chest should not move, only your stomach. Watch to see that only your hand on your stomach goes up as you "fill the balloon with air".
3. Hold your breath while you keep the balloon filled with air and say **Relax** to yourself.
4. Slowly breathe out through your nose counting to 3. The balloon in your stomach will get smaller when you breathe out, and the hand on your stomach should go down.
5. Hold your breath and say **Relax** to yourself.

Each time your child practises Deep Breathing they must blow the imaginary balloon UP and DOWN in their stomach at least 5 times.

Activity

Write down times when your child could use Deep Breathing to keep CALM?

____

How would you know that your child needed to use Deep Breathing to keep CALM?

____

Write down how you could prompt your child to use Deep Breathing?

____

Keep Calm
Parent 2

Take Action

The second way to keep CALM is to practise Move My Muscles Relaxation.

Relaxation works really well in getting rid of the tightness in your child's muscles. Relaxing their muscles will make your child feel CALM and not worry about their Anxious Body Signals. In this Relaxation exercise, your child needs to tense and then relax each muscle from their face to their feet.

This is how your child is being taught to use Relaxation:

1. **FACE:** Screw up your face (including your nose and eyes) and count to 3. Pretend that you have just smelt something really bad. Then say **Relax.**
2. **SHOULDERS:** Shrug your shoulders upwards — try to make them touch your ears — and count to 3. Then say **Relax** to yourself and drop your shoulders down again.
3. **HANDS:** Squeeze your fingers together, like you are squeezing a ball and count to 3. Then say **Relax** to yourself and let your fingers relax.
4. **STOMACH:** Pull your stomach in and pretend you are trying to squeeze through a very small gap in a wall. Count to 3. Then say **Relax** to yourself and push your stomach out again.
5. **LEGS:** Make your legs really straight and tighten all the muscles in your legs. Count to 3. Then say **Relax** to yourself and make your legs all floppy (like a rag doll).
6. **FEET:** Clench and point your toes towards the floor. Count to 3. Then say **Relax** to yourself, roll your feet around in circles and unclench your toes.

Activity

Write down times when your child could use Relaxation to keep CALM?

____

How would you know that your child needed to use Relaxation to keep CALM?

____

Write down how you could prompt your child to use Relaxation?

____

Take Action

Keep Calm
Parent 3

ACTION Parents Can Take

You have learnt two ways to help your child to keep CALM. Encourage your child to practise their Deep Breathing and Muscle Relaxation whenever they are AWARE of feeling anxious! It is important that parents are AWARE of their child's Anxious Feelings and Body Signals so that children can be prompted to keep CALM.

Ways for your child to feel good

It is important that your child does other 'feel good' activities so that they can learn that there are other positive feelings to experience in life.

Below is a list of things that often make children feel good. Tick the activities that your child could do to feel good. Most of these activities have been chosen as they are relatively low cost to families. Add any other OPTIONS you can THINK of to the end of the list.

Household activities

- ☐ Listening to music
- ☐ Quiet time alone
- ☐ Reading
- ☐ Sleeping
- ☐ Art — drawing, painting, crafts
- ☐ Using Stress ball
- ☐ "Pleasures book" — lists or pictures of things that make your child happy
- ☐ Watching TV shows
- ☐ Playing games — computer games, card games, board games
- ☐ Writing a letter or email to a relative
- ☐ Doing puzzles
- ☐ Talking to a family member, a friend, or a pet — share the problem
- ☐ Help somebody
- ☐ Write things down
- ☐ Doing home plays, playing charades

Social activities

- ☐ Have a sleepover at a friends, or go hang out at their house
- ☐ Rent a movie and make popcorn

Sporting activities

- ☐ Riding a bike
- ☐ Skateboarding or skating
- ☐ Walking or running (taking a pet for a walk)
- ☐ Bouncing on trampoline
- ☐ Throwing a ball around together
- ☐ Playing their favourite sport (e.g. tennis, swimming, basketball)
- ☐ Gardening
- ☐ Dancing

Excursions/community activities

- ☐ Going to the park
- ☐ Fishing
- ☐ Camping
- ☐ Hiking
- ☐ Going to the library
- ☐ Visiting museums or historical buildings
- ☐ Going out for ice-cream or favourite treat
- ☐ Visiting neighbours or relatives
- ☐ Going bowling
- ☐ Collecting rocks/shells/leaves
- ☐ Going to the beach

This page is intentionally blank.

Take Action

Thoughts
Parent 1

THINK Strong Thoughts

Building on from being AWARE and keeping CALM, the third step in the ACTION plan teaches children to THINK positively and confidently. Children will learn strategies for turning Scared (unhelpful) thoughts into Strong (positive) thoughts

Activity

Can you recall a time your child OVERESTIMATED THE RISK/DANGER in a situation?

What was the situation?

____

What happened?

____

____

Can you recall a time your child UNDERESTIMATED THEIR ABILITY TO COPE in a situation?

What was the situation?

____

What happened?

____

____

ACTION Parents Can Take

You can help your child to challenge overestimations of risk and danger by prompting them to look for evidence both for and against their scary thoughts; by helping them devise a coping plan for situations in which they feel they cannot cope, and by helping them to learn that their thoughts are not scary. It is also helpful for parents to monitor their own thoughts and take note of the times they might overestimate risk, underestimate their coping and/or be concerned about their own thoughts. In these cases, it is helpful if parents can refrain from sharing their scared thoughts with children and instead, identify strong thoughts that help children to approach difficult situations with realistic expectations and coping plans.

Take ACTION Parenting Strategies: Increasing Strong behaviour

Parents can assist children in managing their anxiety through the following effective and well-researched strategies:

Be on the look out for Strong behaviour in your child

Keep an eye on what your child is doing and look for times when your child is being Strong. What constitutes Strong behaviour may differ between children, but it might include approaching a situation that has scared them in the past or trying a new activity. Paying attention to Strong behaviour will increase the likelihood that your child will repeat the (Strong) behaviour.

Reward Strong behaviour

It is important to reward your child's Strong behaviour — the behaviour that you want repeated. Try to reward the Strong behaviour with praise and / or physical affection immediately after the behaviour occurs. For example, a parent may give their child a hug and say, "You did really well just then — you were able to talk to that new person for 15 minutes". Praise is very powerful and it helps your child identify their strengths and capabilities.

Praise can include acknowledging your child's efforts in a clear and specific way (e.g., "I noticed you tried hard to keep CALM then, that's great!") and / or showing him/her signs of affection (e.g., smile, nod, hug). Give physical affection to your child when they are being Strong, not to soothe their anxiety. Soothing their anxious behaviour instead of Strong behaviour can inadvertently make children engage in the anxious behaviour more often. Be enthusiastic and express your pleasure in your child's efforts, not just their successes.

A reward or a special privilege can also be given to encourage your child to repeat Strong behaviour. The more you reward Strong behaviour, the less likely it is that your child will engage in anxious behaviour as they will be receiving your attention for positive, Strong behaviour.

Take Action

Thoughts
Parent 2B

Model CALM and Strong behaviour

It is important that parents act as CALM and Strong role models for their children, by keeping CALM, voicing Strong Thoughts (and avoid voicing Scared Thoughts) and approaching situations rather than avoiding them. If a child sees a parent keeping CALM and in control, they are more likely to believe they can take ACTION against their anxiety. Parents should encourage children to behave in a CALM and Strong way, just like them.

Parenting anxious children can be challenging at times. When this is the case, it is important that you are AWARE of your own thoughts and feelings, try to keep CALM and interact with your child in a positive way. Just as children have their own Strong Team, it can be beneficial for parents to speak with family and friends when these challenges arise.

Spend 'feel good' and 'talk time' with your child

Spend quality time with your child doing 'feel good' activities, like reading or playing with them. This will help children to learn that happy times can be experienced.

To help your child manage their own anxiety, encourage them to share their experiences and thoughts with you. Spend time talking with your child about their day and how they can use the steps in the ACTION plan to manage their anxiety. Try not to trivialise a child's fears or concerns. This support and understanding will nurture a sense of trust between yourself and your child. Most importantly, encourage and support your child to approach their fears and concerns and deal with them, rather than avoid them. Also, avoid "solving the problem" for your child by taking the ACTION your child might have needed to take. Always evaluate how your child went when they take ACTION against their anxiety and reward Strong behaviour. Spending 'talk time' with your child will ensure they will be more likely to talk to you about future experiences.

Thoughts
Parent 2C

Take Action

Take ACTION Parenting Strategies: Decreasing anxious behaviour

Refocusing anxious behaviour

In the same way that giving your child attention for being Strong will increase this behaviour, giving attention to anxious behaviour (e.g., excessive talking about the situation, delaying or avoiding the situation) will make it more likely that your child will feel anxious in the situation again. Parents can help refocus anxious behaviour by acknowledging their child's anxiety in the situation, and then prompting them to use the steps in the ACTION plan. Parents can help shift the balance from anxious to Strong behaviour by reminding children about "false alarms", encouraging them to use their Keep CALM and Strong THOUGHTS strategies, and to get INTO Action by taking small steps to deal with their fears.

Make a plan

It is also helpful to make a clear plan with your child about situations that warrant reassurance (i.e., 'real' alarms) versus those that do not (i.e., 'false' alarms). Encourage your child to ask themselves "which one is it" before they come to you for reassurance, and let them know your job is to help them to Take Action. Encourage them to reassure themselves with Strong thoughts. Sometimes, this might mean ignoring reassurance seeking and using praise for Strong behaviour to refocus anxiety.

Avoid excessive reassurance

It is useful for parents to reassure their child that they can act in a Strong way (e.g., keep CALM and THINK Strong thoughts). However, excessive reassurance is less helpful to children because they may then believe they need this reassurance each time the situation occurs. Also, excessive reassurance only relieves anxiety in the short-term and the time taken to provide additional reassurance can delay taking Action. Once you have reassured your child, refocus anxious behaviour by prompting them to use the steps in the Action plan.

Be consistent

It is important that you are consistent with the Take ACTION parenting strategies. It is important to let other family members know about the strategies you will be using to decrease your child's anxious behaviour, so consistency takes place across settings as well.

Take Action

Into Action
Parent 1

Get INTO Action

The fourth step in the ACTION plan encourages children to gradually confront anxiety-provoking situations using an ACTION Ladder (a step-by-step exposure hierarchy).

Why is it important for your child to practise and approach scary situations?

Children who are anxious often engage in safety behaviours (e.g., gain excessive reassurance; be highly organised; carry a lucky charm) and avoidance of scary situations.

Consequences of safety behaviours include:

- Children believe that they cannot approach situations without engaging in the safety behaviour. For example, a child who worries a lot about doing well at school might not be able to take a test unless they have studied excessively beforehand. This increases the likelihood that they will engage in the safety behaviour again next time.
- If children do approach the scary situation, they are likely to attribute any success to the safety behaviour. For example, a child who worries a lot about being late for school might always want their parents to take a certain route to school. Being on time is then attributed to taking that route — the safety behaviour — when in reality they were unlikely to run late regardless of the route taken.

Consequences of avoiding scary situations include:

- The fear is strengthened or reinforced. For example, a child who avoids spiders will continue to perceive spiders as scary.
- Children miss out on learning opportunities that might disprove or disconfirm their Scared Thoughts and provide evidence to support Strong Thoughts. For example, a child who avoids reading in front of the class will not learn that they can cope with this situation and do a good job!
- Children miss the opportunity to practise developmentally appropriate skills. For example, a child who avoids speaking with peers will not gain practice in conversation skills. Children need to be reminded that people develop confidence by frequently practising their skills (e.g., elite sportspeople) and learning from their mistakes.

ACTION Parents Can Take

Parents can assist their child by validating their fears (e.g., "I can see you are feeling scared at the moment...") but avoiding excessive verbal reassurance. This can inadvertently enable your child to delay dealing with the feared situation. Try to acknowledge your child's fears and encourage them to take ACTION (without their safety behaviours). You can help remind your child about the importance of approaching situations, instead of avoiding them.

Into Action
Parent 2A

Take Action

There are several key features to creating a successful ACTION Ladder

1. One step at a time

The first step in the ACTION Ladder must be something that your child can do already. It is better to err on the side of choosing a situation which is easier than expected, rather than choosing something daunting and your child feeling unable to proceed, or feeling overwhelmed. Fears can be made worse if a child suddenly forces himself or herself, without sufficient preparation, to confront something that has been avoided or which is perceived as extremely threatening. The steps on the ACTION Ladder should not be too far apart and must be achievable during the Take Action program.

2. Stay until CALM

It is very important that your child remains in the situation until their anxiety begins to decrease. Children should feel Cool on the Feelometer before leaving the situation. Children may get worried about this and THINK "How bad could the anxiety get?" Remember anxiety only increases to a certain level and then declines, even when children do not use calming strategies to help this process. Children must stay in the scary situation until they feel CALM so they learn that they can cope and the situation is not that scary — they just THINK it is! Your child needs to practise the skills in the ACTION plan, especially Keep CALM and using Strong Thoughts, while climbing their ACTION Ladder.

Take Action

Into Action
Parent 2B

3. Practise often – First time, Second time, Third time

Just confronting a situation once will not be enough to take away your child's anxiety completely. It takes many repetitions, as well as using the skills in the ACTION Plan, to "wear down" the anxiety associated with a given situation. This frequent practise will result in your child feeling less and less anxious in the same situation. The more frequently a situation is confronted the sooner the degree of anxiety will begin to reduce. Remember that approaching and practising the skills in the ACTION Plan when in scary situations decreases anxiety.

4. Practise in lots of situations and with lots of different stimuli that trigger anxiety.

For example, if your child is afraid of vomiting, they could practise eating food from the food court in a local shopping centre; at a birthday party; and the deli. They could do high impact exercise that increases physical arousal. Your child could also practise with a variety of feared foods, such as crunchy and lumpy textures, reheated food, and any food items they specifically avoid. The key message is that practising the ACTION Plan in lots of situations and with lots of stimuli that triggers fear is likely to strengthen anxiety reductions.

Into Action
Parent 3

Take Action

Obstacles in creating an ACTION Ladder

ACTION Ladders are one of the most important strategies learnt in the Take ACTION Program. It is important to THINK about what obstacles may hinder your child's progress in climbing their ACTION Ladder. Tick which of the following obstacles below may be relevant for you and your child.

Activity

☐ Safety behaviours e.g., excessive reassurance (please describe)

____

☐ Avoidance (please describe)

____

☐ Communicating your own fears to your child (please describe)

____

☐ Your child not completing the entire step on the ACTION Ladder (please describe)

____

☐ Your child not practising often enough (please describe)

____

☐ Your child not staying in the situation until CALM (please describe)

____

☐ Appropriate rewards (please describe)

____

☐ Worries that this might cause the distress in your child (please describe)

____

ACTION Parents Can Take

Be AWARE of these obstacles over the coming weeks and use the Take ACTION strategies to overcome the obstacles. Remember the more your child takes ACTION, the faster their anxiety will decrease.

Take Action

Options
Parent 1A

O Use my OPTIONS

The fifth step in the ACTION plan teaches children additional strategies (or OPTIONS) to further manage their anxiety.

Activity

The first OPTION is Problem Solving

Children learn to solve problems by thinking about the best ACTION to take. They record a Scared thought in the Option One bubble and what ACTION he/she would take. Then they write a Strong Thought in Option 2 and what ACTION he/she would take. They learn to solve problems by weighing up their ACTIONS. Encourage your child to follow these steps when they have a problem. Write the situation in the box below and follow the Problem Solving steps.

1. Thought OPTIONS List two of the thoughts your child could have about this scary time.	**2. What type of thought is this (scared; strong)?**	**3. What ACTION would your child take if he/she thought this way?**

Option One

Option Two

Options
Parent 1B

Take Action

4. Weigh up the OPTIONS — What is the best Option for your child to choose (Look at the ACTION column to decide)?____________________
5. Take ACTION — Your child needs to act out the best Option. (Look at the Action column to decide).

The remaining handouts used for Parents in the
Use my OPTIONS step are the same as child handouts:

- Options Child 3
- Options Child 4
- Options Child 5
- Options Child 6
- Options Child 7
- Options Child 8
- Options Child 10 (A, B, C)
- Options Child 11
- Options Child 14

The remaining handouts used for Parents in the
NEVER stop taking ACTION step are the same as child handouts:

- NEVER stop taking ACTION Child 1
- NEVER stop taking ACTION Child 2A, B

Appendix C
Home Task Sheets

Home Task Reward Chart

Home Task One

Home Task Two

Home Task Three

Home Task Parent

Home Task Four

Home Task Five

Home Task Six

Home Task Seven

Home Task Eight

Home Task Nine

Take Action

Home Task Reward Chart

Home Task Reward Chart

Every time you complete a Home Task, you will receive a tick in the box that matches that week's Home Task. See if you can earn all the ticks by the end of the Take Action program.

Session	Home Tasks Assigned	Tick Completed	Therapist's Signature
1			
2	One, Two		
3	Three, Parent Task		
4	Three, Four		
5	Three, Five		
6	Three, Six, Seven		
7	Three, Six, Seven		
8	Three, Six, Seven, Eight		
9	Three, Six, Seven, Eight, Nine		
10			

Be Aware
Home Task One

Take Action

Home Task One
Rewards Menu

It is important that you are rewarded for doing your Home Tasks. Here's an example of a Reward Menu:

Home Task Number	Reward
1	10 minutes to spend on favourite activity
2	Favourite snack
3	20 minutes to spend on favourite activity
4	Getting your favourite dinner
5	Getting a stress ball
6	Getting a new writing book
7	Getting a new game
8	Going on a family picnic
9	Going to the movies
10	Trip to a theme park

Talk to your parents about what rewards you would like for completing your Home Tasks. Remember rewards are not only money or other material things. Rewards can be things that you like to do (e.g. special outings) or things that make you feel good (e.g. playing the computer) or even telling yourself you've done a good job.

Write down the rewards in the table below. Remember you will receive one tick each time you complete a Home Task. Ask your parent/s to sign underneath the Rewards Menu. You can earn smaller rewards throughout the program, or you can save your ticks for a larger reward (e.g. trip to a theme park after earning 10 ticks).

My Rewards Menu

Home Task Number	Reward
1	
2	
3	
4	
5	
6	
7	
8	
9	
10	

I agree with ________________ (child's name) Reward Menu and will be able to provide these rewards for ______________ (child's name)

Parent's Signature: ______________________

Home Task Two

Write down a time that you felt each of the emotions below:

1. Happy or Excited

Rate your level on the Feelometer:

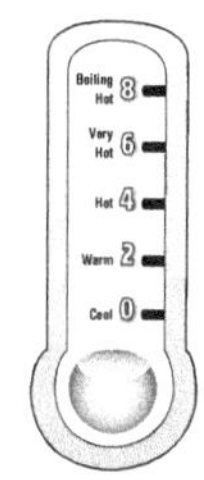

____

How did you know that you felt happy or excited (e.g. I was smiling):

____

2. Anxious

Rate your level on the Feelometer:

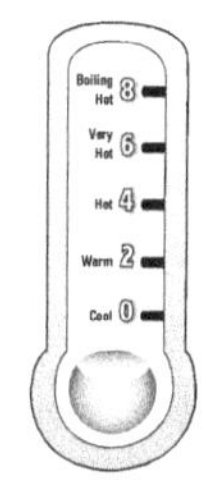

____

How did you know that you felt anxious (e.g. my heart was beating fast):

____

3. CALM and Relaxed

Rate your level on the Feelometer:

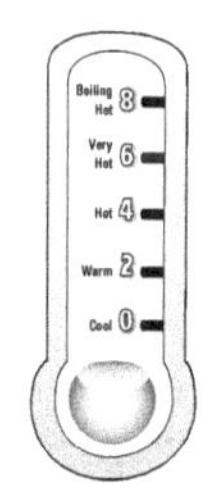

____

How did you know that you felt calm and relaxed (e.g. I was laughing with my friends):

____

____

Take Action

Home Task Three

On the Spot Deep Breathing and Move My Muscles Relaxation Practice

For each day of the week shown below, tick the box if you practised your Breathing and Relaxation. Write down your rating on the Feelometer before and after doing your Breathing and Relaxation (Sunday is practise-free!).

	Monday	Tuesday	Wednesday	Thursday	Friday	Saturday
Tick if you did your Deep Breathing						
Rating on Feelometer before Breathing						
Rating on Feelometer after Breathing						
Tick if you did your Muscle Relaxation						
Rating on Feelometer before Relaxation						
Rating on Feelometer after Relaxation						

Take Action

Keep Calm
Home Task Parent

Home Task

Parent Monitoring Diary

Use the Parent Monitoring Diary below to help understand your child's anxiety better.

Date & Time	Describe the anxious situation	Rating of child's anxiety on Feelometer	What showed you that your child was anxious (e.g. Body Signals)?	What did your child do (e.g., avoid) or say?	What did you do or say?

This page is intentionally blank.

Home Task Four

Catching Scared Thoughts

In this Home Task, catch some Scared Thoughts you had during the week and write them in the table below.
If you do not have any Scared Thoughts this week, THINK about scary times you have had over the past few weeks or months and then fill in the table.

	Example	My Scary Time	My Scary Time
What happened?	I had to give a talk in my class		
What Anxious Body Signals did you have?	Fast beating heart and butterflies in my stomach.		
How did you feel?	Scared		
Rating on the Feelometer	Boiling Hot		
What Scared Thoughts did you have?	The other kids will laugh at me. I will forget what I have to say.		
What ACTION did you take?	I told my mum that I felt sick so I didn't have to go to school		

This page is intentionally blank.

Take Action

Thoughts
Home Task Five

Home Task Five

Strength Cards

THINK of a Scared Thought you have had recently.

What was the Scared Thought you had? ______________________________

____

How did the Scared Thought make you feel? ______________________________

____

What Anxious Body Signals did you have? ______________________________

____

Rating on the Feelometer: ______________________________

Write the Scared Thought on Side 1 of your Strength Card.

SIDE 1 **Scared Thought**

THINK of a Strong Thought that you can use to weaken the Scared Thought.
Write the Strong Thought on Side 2 of your Strength Card.

SIDE 2 **Strong Thought**

This page is intentionally blank.

Take Action

Into Action
Home Task Six

Home Task Six

Reviewing my ACTION Plan

Let's review how things went while you completed a step on your ACTION Ladder. Remember to use all the skills in the ACTION plan while you are practising each step.

Write down the step on your ACTION Ladder on the lines below.

____

____

A

Be AWARE:

How did you feel before doing this step on your ACTION Ladder?

What Anxious Body Signals did you have? ____________________

____

Rating on the Feelometer before practising this step: ____________

C

Keep CALM:

How did you keep CALM while practising this step? ____________

____

T

THINK Strong Thoughts:

Write down the Scared Thoughts that you had: ________________

____

Write down the Strong Thoughts that you had: __________________

____

I

Get INTO Action:

When did you practise this step on your ACTION Ladder? __________

____

My reward for climbing this step is: __________________________

Rating on the Feelometer after practising this step: ____________

O

N

Home Task Seven

Reviewing my ACTION Ladder

Write down the step you completed on your ACTION Ladder:

____

THINK about how you went climbing this step on your ACTION Ladder. On the blackboard below, write down the things that went well when you practised this step.

Things that went well

THINK about the things that you could try to improve for the next step on your ACTION Ladder. On the blackboard below, write down the things that you could do differently on the next step.

Things I could improve next time

When you climb the next step on your ACTION Ladder, do the things you have written above. Remember to use all the skills in the ACTION plan as well!

Home Task Eight
Being Assertive Practice

Look for a time when you could practise being Strong, Confident and Assertive and answer the questions below.

Write down when you were Confident and Assertive (like the Strong Dolphin) on the line below:

____

Step One: Tell the other person what you think the problem is

Step Two: Tell the other person how you feel about the problem

Step Three: Tell the other person a solution to the problem

Did you use Confident Body Signals (SMILE)? ☐ **YES** ☐ **NO**

Write down how you felt and what happened after you were Confident and Assertive on the lines below:

____

____

Take Action

Home Task Nine

Being Assertive Practice

Answer the questions below if a time comes up when you need to use the steps for Dealing with Bullying.

Write down when you had to deal with bullying on the line below:

____

Step One: ______________________________________

Step Two: Circle which Strong and Confident OPTIONS you chose

Walk away

Tell an adult

Ignore the bullying if you can

Say "I heard what you said and I don't really care"

Tell them firmly and calmly to leave you alone

Imagine there is a force field all around you protecting you from their words

Step Three: Did you decide on the best Option and take ACTION?

____

Congratulate yourself for dealing with this situation!

Write down how you felt and what happened after you used the Steps for Dealing with Bullying:

____

____

www.ingramcontent.com/pod-product-compliance
Lightning Source LLC
LaVergne TN
LVHW080044210926
848481LV00011B/3279
* 9 7 8 1 9 2 2 1 1 7 2 7 4 *